CITIES ON THE MOVE

Urban Chaos and Global Change
East Asian Art, Architecture and Film Now

Hayward Gallery

Published on the occasion of *Cities on the Move: Urban Chaos and Global Change – East Asian Art, Architecture and Film Now*, organised by the Hayward Gallery, London, 13 May – 27 June 1999, in collaboration with Secession Vienna and capcMusée d'art contemporain de Bordeaux

Exhibition tour
Secession Vienna
26 November 1997 – 18 January 1998
capcMusée d'art contemporain de Bordeaux
5 June – 30 August 1998
PS1 New York
18 October 1998 – 10 January 1999
Louisiana Museum of Modern Art, Humlebaek, Denmark
29 January – 21 April 1999
Kiasma Museum of Contemporary Art, Helsinki
5 November – 19 December 1999

Exhibition curated by Hou Hanru and Hans-Ulrich Obrist
Hayward Gallery exhibition organised by Fiona Bradley, assisted by Julia Coates and Sophie Allen

Catalogue edited by Fiona Bradley, and designed by Stephen Coates and Anne Odling-Smee at August Media.
Photography by Elisabeth Scheder-Bieschin (pp. 21–25, 28–29, 34–40, 43–46, 48, 54, 60, 64, 68 and cover)
Catalogue production coordinated by Uwe Kraus GmbH
Printed in Italy by Musumeci

Front cover: Chen Zhen, *Precipitous Parturition*, 1999 (detail)

Published by Hayward Gallery Publishing, London SE1 8XX

ISBN 1 85332 192 3

Hayward Gallery, National Touring Exhibitions and Arts Council Collection publications are distributed by
Cornerhouse Publications,
70 Oxford Street, Manchester M1 5NH
tel. 0161 200 1503; fax. 0161 200 1504;
email publications@cornerhouse.org.

Contents

Preface

Susan Ferleger Brades, Director, Hayward Gallery

No region in the world has undergone such profound and rapid economic and cultural change as East Asia in the last decade. Poised between reaction and modernity, extreme poverty and supreme wealth, East Asian cities epitomize the concept of 'urban chaos', responding constantly to technological innovations and economic challenges. *Cities on the Move* tracks the cultural impact of East Asian urban development, presenting art, architecture and film in an intense and energetic, constantly changing exhibition.

Cities on the Move opened at the Secession Vienna in November 1997 and since then has travelled to the capcMusée d'art contemporain in Bordeaux, PS1 in New York (in part) and the Louisiana Museum of Modern Art in Denmark before arriving at the Hayward Gallery and going on to Kiasma in Helsinki. Conceived in the midst of urban and financial expansion, the exhibition must today be viewed in the context of economic collapse across the region. Intrinsically dynamic, *Cities on the Move* responds to this, taking in its stride the shifting situation of contemporary East Asian urbanism.

Cities on the Move was curated by Hans-Ulrich Obrist and Hou Hanru. Both have been responsible for a number of major international exhibitions, including *Nuit Blanche* (Musée d'art moderne de la ville de Paris) and *DO IT* (touring throughout Europe, Asia and the USA) (both Hans-Ulrich Obrist) and *Parisien(ne)s* at the Camden Arts Centre in London in 1997 (Hou Hanru). As an evolving project, *Cities on the Move* has made unprecedented demands on the curators' time and initiative and has called for their continued input and expertise. We are particularly grateful for their efforts in reformulating the exhibition for the Hayward Gallery and for London.

The tremendous, speculative ambition of *Cities on the Move* has been enhanced by the dynamic approach to the exhibition's installation at the Hayward by architects Rem Koolhaas and Ole Scheeren. Using the remnants of previous architectural designs for Hayward exhibitions, notably that by Zaha Hadid for *Addressing the Century: 100 Years of Art & Fashion*, they have created an 'event city' for the exhibition: a shifting cityscape of urban possibility. We are honoured to welcome Rem Koolhaas to the Hayward, and we extend our wholehearted thanks to him and to Ole Scheeren. Our thanks also go to Fox Displays, to John Johnson and his crew at Lightwaves, and to Jem Legh, Tom Cullen and Adrian Fogarty for their help with the audio-visual component.

We are also immensely grateful to Nick Barley, Stephen Coates and their team at August Media for designing and developing this catalogue with flair and panache. 'London on the Move', a special section tracking the impact of East Asia on the cultural life of London, was the brainchild of August Media, and we thank them and its author Julia Diamantis. We are again grateful to the exhibition's curators, to Rem Koolhaas and to Mohsen Mostafavi, Chairman of the Architectural Association, for their insightful contributions to the catalogue. Our thanks also go to Elisabeth Scheder-Bieschin for her photographs of the exhibition at the Louisiana Museum of Modern Art.

An exhibition about cities, *Cities on the Move* is inevitably in conversation with London. We have endeavoured to extend this dialogue, pushing the boundaries of the exhibition out into the city, and in doing this we have benefited from the advice of a great many people. We are especially grateful to Kathryn Findlay and John Norden of Ushida Findlay, Peter Murray of Wordsearch Communications, Mohsen Mostafavi and Mark Cousins at the Architectural Association, Ricky Burdett at LSE, Gilane Tawadros and Melanie Keen at inIVA, and Suzanne Marston of Visiting Arts. We are also grateful to Blueprint, our media sponsor, for their creative partnership.

Cities on the Move has benefited throughout its travels from the expertise of individuals in its host institutions. The exhibition was initially organised by the Vienna Secession and the capcMusée d'art contemporain de Bordeaux. We thank Werner Würtinger, Kerstin Scheuch and Christine Bruckbauer, and Henry-Claude Cousseau, Marie-Laure Bernadac and Jean Marc Avrila, respectively, for their advice throughout, as we do Steingrim Laursen, Kjeld Kjeldsen and Åsa Nacking at the Louisiana Museum of Modern Art in Denmark.

The coordination of a project as alive and complex as *Cities on the Move* presents particular challenges to the home team. I would especially like to thank Fiona Bradley, the Hayward's Exhibition Organiser for the show, for so creatively and good-humouredly attending to the myriad details involved in realizing the exhibition here; Martin Caiger-Smith, the Hayward's Head of Exhibitions, for his engagement and commitment; Amanda Hogg for developing a dynamic educational programme; Alex Hinton and Alison Wright for their marketing and press initiatives; Linda Schofield and Lise Connellan for expertly producing this catalogue; and Keith Hardy, Mark King, Steve Cook and the Hayward crew for skilfully meeting the exhibition's complex installation needs.

Above all, we thank the artists and architects who have been involved in *Cities on the Move*, many of whom have travelled to London to work on the installation of the exhibition. A hugely challenging show, it has required their ongoing involvement and attention. We are proud to present their work, and grateful to them for their energy and enthusiasm in making *Cities on the Move* at the Hayward Gallery.

Antonio Sant'Elia, preparatory drawing for 'Città Nuova', 1914

Cities of Distraction

Mohsen Mostafavi

Western imagination has long been dominated by speed. The Italian Futurists, probably more than any other group of artists, placed an emphasis on the pleasures of accelerated mobility. In their first manifesto of 1909, Marinetti declared: 'We say that the world's magnificence has been enriched by a new beauty; the beauty of speed.' Sant'Elia, the visionary architect of the group, imagined a 'new city', the main element of which was a central station not only for trains but also for aeroplanes, trams, buses, cars and pedestrians. Industrial modernization reached its imaginary peak in Sant'Elia's mechanized city. The 'new city' was part of a nodal system of flows whose movements challenged the immobility of the urban monuments of the past.

Although a part of the prophecies and desires of the Futurists has been realized, the passion for speed remains as strong today as it was at the beginning of the century, when cars, trains and planes retained their novelty value as icons of industrial progress. And yet, ironically, the proliferation over the years of the mechanisms of mobility has led to the self-inflicted urban wounds of retardation and congestion. This situation is particularly acute in a growing number of East Asian cities.

Development in East Asia, as in other places, is defined by the intersection of local, regional and global forces of culture, politics and capital. Since the Second World War, however, East Asian city landscapes have for the most part been more radically and more visibly transformed than their Western counterparts. This can be attributed largely to East Asia's embrace of various processes of modernization, but each country's political and economic history (colonialism, nationalism, military rule, ethnic migration, etc.) also directly affects its role, and its capabilities, within the larger regional and global network. While these cities are in themselves unique they nevertheless exhibit certain similar features.

In these cities, congestion is further exacerbated by the rapid growth of the urban population, as people migrate from rural areas in search of new opportunities. In Hong Kong, the congestion of bodies in space makes the crowds in London seem almost sparse by comparison. Congestion produces a range of side effects. It results in the need to accommodate greater numbers of people on land that is invariably scarce. An increase in density often goes hand in hand with a reduction in the size of the dwelling units. At the same time, it can lead to the formation of new models for their aggregation, which can vary from fast-track techniques of design and construction to projects that occur outside of established regulatory frameworks. The speed of urbanization in parts of China or Korea, where new cities with populations approaching a million inhabitants have been built over a few years, attests to the impact of global financial networks that simultaneously exploit and benefit East Asian cities. The condition of congestion exaggerates the distinction between rich and poor through an ever closer juxtaposition of their different worlds. The hybrid effects of modernization, combining Western attitudes with East Asian values, confront urban populations whose origins are largely proto-rural or pre-industrial.

The transformations that are taking place in East Asian cities do not, however, fit the historic duality between modernity and tradition, for in many ways they are triggered as much by telecommunications systems as they are by industrial modernization. The instantaneity of the virtual super highway has supplanted the speed of Sant'Elia's 'new city'.

Telecommunications systems allow global access to financial markets and in turn provide the basic framework for local economic development. The global and the local, the present and the past, are deeply intertwined. For example, Tokyo's 5000-plus local convenience stores are linked via a network that logistically analyses their stock and sales patterns with great accuracy, allowing them to remain competitive in a highly decentralized market. The responsiveness of particular markets leads to a form of nomadism, allowing retailers to quickly shrink or expand their operations in particular areas. But, more importantly, bar-code systems, such as UPC (Universal Product Code) and the Japanese Pointed Operations System, have become the registers, through consumption, of group patterns of behaviour that transcend specific cultures, communities or localities. (Equally, these systems allow manufacturers to monitor and control the global distribution of branded goods and to create new networks of allegiance amongst consumers.)

In the absence of both real opportunities for political engagement and long-term provisions of social structure, many people in East Asian cities have 'invested' their future in various forms of financial speculation in the property and stock markets. The self-image of these city-dwellers is forged through international patterns of fashion and consumerism. The uneven modernity of the present is further affected by new means of electronic media which, according to Arjun Appadurai, 'transform the field of mass mediation because they offer new resources and new disciplines for the construction of imagined selves and imagined worlds'.[1] Images from afar are brought closer in ways that overcome national or local boundaries; they create mobile identities that are no longer fixed to particular concepts of region or territory. In the age of mass media, identities are de-territorialized, hybridized and constantly shifting. The electronic society engenders new 'wish-landscapes' through tourism and migration. But the fluidity, flexibility and decentralization which are often cited as the

1. Arjun Appadurai, 1997, *Modernity at Large: Cultural Dimensions of Globalization*, University of Minnesota, Minneapolis, p. 3.

hallmarks of the new virtual global economy do not always find their equivalence in physical space.

Cities on the Move is an evolving body of work, dealing with art, architecture, urbanism, film and writing in relation to East Asian cities. The exhibition does not present a unitary vision of development; it uncovers a plurality of ideas and approaches – ideas that are inevitably circumstantial, conflictual and ephemeral. It is in the transient nature of things that we must look for clues about the workings of the agents of change.

In his recent book, *Hong Kong: Culture and the Politics of Disappearance*, Ackbar Abbas speaks of the 'relationship of disappearance to speed, the kind of speed that comes in the wake of electronic technology and the mediatization of the real, and the spatial distortions produced by this kind of speed'.[2] The physical and dynamic transformations that are taking place in many East Asian cities, like the changes in global cities, are often directly affected by the inter-relationship between the virtual and the real, where, according to Paul Virilio in his book *The Lost Dimension*, 'direct and mediated perceptions merge into an instantaneous representation of space and the surrounding environment'.[3]

Cities on the Move pays homage to what Siegfried Kracauer called 'the cult of distraction' in his essay of 1926 on Berlin's Picture Palaces. For Kracauer, distraction was a mode of emphasizing the externality of things, the reading of their surface; a form of alertness under conditions of discontinuity: 'aesthetic representation is the more real the less it cuts itself off from the reality outside it'.[4] The everyday and the trivial are re-valued as legitimate components of culture. The partial and fragmentary nature of the development of East Asian cities is paralleled in the selection of materials on show. The exhibition is an analogous city made anew with the accumulated traces of economic and cultural debris; of what has been and what is yet to come.

In the context of London, *Cities on the Move* performs the urgent task of demonstrating some of the more specific consequences of the space that lies between globalization and colonialism. Globalization can, in one sense, be viewed as reframing old colonial power relations, albeit without the necessity for actual physical occupation of territory – except that global cities such as London or New York are themselves now being colonized by people whose countries have been physically or economically colonized by the West. This reverse pattern of migration suggests that many global cities will increasingly need to address issues of racial, ethnic and cultural difference – issues that have already deeply affected many East Asian cities. The city, as the contested site of difference, becomes an important domain for challenging the essentially economic forms of distributive justice. The city must therefore provide spatially democratic frameworks which will support its citizens in order to construct new identities based on difference. *Cities on the Move* shows traits – some spectacularly inspiring, some disconcerting – that need to be included in future debates on the global city.

2. Ackbar Abbas, 1997, *Hong Kong: Culture and the Politics of Disappearance*, Hong Kong University Press, Hong Kong, p. 9.

3. Paul Virilio, 1991, *The Lost Dimension*, Semiotext(e), New York, pp. 30-31.

4. Siegfried Kracauer, *Das Ornament der Masse*, pp. 54-55, quoted in Thomas Elsaesser, 'The Irresponsible Signifier' in *New German Critique*, New York, no. 4, Winter 1987, p. 82. See also in the same issue 'Cult of Distraction: On Berlin Picture Palaces', pp. 91-96.

Cities on the Move

Hou Hanru and Hans-Ulrich Obrist

Cities on the Move presents the dynamic and highly creative situation of contemporary urban visual culture in East Asia. Art, architecture and urbanism are explored as manifestations of the process of modernization in the region – a modernization which is not only regionally important but also globally significant.

Now, at the end of the twentieth century, economic, political and cultural life in East Asia is undergoing rapid change. The established economic powers of Japan, Hong Kong, Singapore, South Korea and Taiwan are being joined by newly developing economies in China, Malaysia, Thailand, Indonesia, the Philippines, Vietnam and elsewhere. The region has witnessed a spectacular process of economic and social progress, the signs of which are most obvious in the pace of construction. Urban space has expanded, and new cities have emerged all over the Asian Pacific region. Typical examples are China's 'Special Economic Zones' such as Shenzhen, Zhuhai and the Pudong Area of Shanghai, where thousands of high-rise buildings have been erected on land which was, until very recently, under agricultural use.

Rapid urbanization calls for high-speed construction. The unprecedented speed at which new urban areas develop in Asia, the metropolitan present thrusting violently into the immediate rural past, brings together local and internationally-renowned foreign architects, attracted by the dynamism of the Asian urban situation. A process of confrontation and exchange between architects within Asia and beyond has generated some innovative and controversial models of architectural/urban practice which are specific to Asia.

Culture, in such a context, is by nature hybrid, impure and contradictory. As new cities are built, and existing cities expanded, renovated and transformed, signs of different cultures are emphasized in order to celebrate globalization. The development of Asian urban areas appears to follow the architect Rem Koolhaas' concept of 'Cities of Exacerbated Difference', developed in his influential Harvard Design School Project on the Pearl River Delta in 1997: 'In the Pearl River Delta, we are confronted with a new urban system. It will never become a city in the recognizable sense of the word. Each part is both competitive with and has a relationship to each other part. Now these parts are being stitched together by infrastructures so that every part is connected, but not into a whole. We call this new model the City of Exacerbated Difference (COED). A city that does not imply the stability of a definitive configuration because each part is fixed, unstable and in a state of perpetual mutual adjustment defining themselves in relation to all other parts.'

An irreconcilable contradiction can be seen within the pragmatic belief (promoted as an official ideology of development in 'modernized' Asia) in the cooperation between Asian lifestyles and social mores and a global, liberal consumer economy. The official image of post-colonial, post-dictatorship modernization in the region is in line with the pursuit of economic power common throughout the developed world. However, an inevitable tension exists between the desire for a capitalist economy and the traditions of Asian culture. Most Asian countries have opted for modernization of the national economy and culture in the belief that this will lead to independence. However, more often, the desire for a modern, Western economy leads to a paternalistic structure of social management, and to the perverse pursuit of 'hyper-capitalism'. Currently, East Asia exists in a state of permanent and frenzied transformation, with almost unbearable urban density, uncontrollably rapid economic expansion, profligate exploitation of natural and human resources and the loss of social, cultural and political stability as the new conditions of existence.

Consumerism is the predominant symptom of the East Asian modernization explosion. Any Asian urban society, be it politically traditional or communist, is now a consumer society, in which values and human relationships are increasingly subsumed in material and monetary exchanges. As a symbol of this, almost every major city in the region has constructed, with the backing of national, municipal and private corporations, monumental commercial edifices: complexes of offices, shopping malls, entertainment centres and international hotels. Thus Hong Kong has Time Square and Pacific Place, Kuala Lumpur has Sunway Lagoon, Singapore the Great Wall City, Beijing has the New Dongan Centre, and so on. Each authority's ultimate goal is to offer their city the tallest building in the world in celebration of progress and successful modernization. Currently, Kuala Lumpur is the proud possessor of the Petronas Twin Tower (450 metres high), designed by Cesar Pelli. Its status as the world's tallest building will be overturned in a few month's time with the completion of the Shanghai World Financial Centre, designed by KPF Associates.

This type of competitive urbanism has given rise to a style of Asian corporate architecture, symptomatic of another concept advanced by Koolhaas, that of the 'Generic City'. East Asian cities are key points in a network of such cities across the world, which influence and perhaps even dictate a new, homogenised, urban world order. Acknowledgement of their place in such a network has led Asian cities to construct huge monuments to modern transport: Osaka, Hong Kong, Kuala Lumpur and Shanghai have the world's newest and largest airports, designed by architects Renzo Piano, Norman Foster, Kisho Kurokawa and Paul Andreu. Real networking is supplemented by virtual, as new urban areas are planned and developed as Asian 'silicon valleys' – Malaysia has a 'Multimedia Super Corridor' responsible, along with Taiwan, Korea,

Armin Linke
Installation shots from *Cities on the Move* in Vienna, Bordeaux, New York and Denmark
© the artist 1999
[all photographs, pp. 11–13]

Singapore and China, for the production of most of the computers in the global market. The most advanced telecommunications technologies have now become a 'natural' part of everyday East Asian urban life, as mobile phones, email and the internet are not only trendy gadgets for young people to show off but also indispensable tools for urban survival.

A new Asian middle class is emerging within these global cities. Dynamic in action, ambitious in politics, open to the new and anxious for urban sophistication, they are the ideal consumers of the cultural products of the new global market. However, as the first Asian modern middle class generation they are also profoundly conservative in social terms, keen to establish for themselves a secure financial status. The product of a post-colonial economy and culture, they are a hybrid of Westernized modernism and nationalist tradition. Theirs is the dominant influence on the configuration of Asian cities, their aesthetic preferences the driving force in the creation of new urban spaces and imagery. Their goal is the combination of the most advanced architectural know-how with the traditional ideals of 'Asian identity'; this leads to a kind of in-between architectural style in which to encapsulate an Asian, non-western brand of modernization. This results, all too often, in an approach to urban space reminiscent of the theme park – many Asian cities have a policy for the systematic recreation of 'history' and the refurbishment of 'indigenous' culture along the lines of Disneyland or Las Vegas. Paradoxically, the result of such initiatives is the disappearance of real historic areas, flattened to make way for hyper-'real' simulacras of tradition. Originally intended to attract tourists to East Asia, these reconstructed histories have become an integral part of contemporary urban life, a guarantee of the 'globality' of an East Asian city. In Singapore's China Town, for example, visitors and locals may enjoy a district restored and painted in dazzling colours to recall its own fantastic and exotic past, indistinguishable from its counterparts in any Disneyland. Its centrepiece, the recently completed Far East Square, combines Feng Shui principles with high-tech glass and steel construction techniques to enact a clash of post-colonial civilizations and identities.

The architects and artists represented in *Cities on the Move* engage specifically with the challenges of the contemporary East Asian urban condition. Some architects, such as Tay Kheng Soon, Ken Yeang, Toyo Ito, Itsuko Hasegawa and William Lim seek to accommodate ecological concerns within the most high-tech constructions, allowing new cities to 'breathe' in the rhythm of their recently rural identities. Others, such as Rem Koolhaas with his masterplanning of Hanoi New Town and Arata Isozaki with his Mirage City of 1996, are feeling their way towards a new utopia, a 'Generic City' of global confluence, a 'tourbillon in which the West wind and the East wind encounter each other' (Isozaki). At the same time, a younger generation of architects is concentrating on more flexible strategies of negotiation directly with urban density and hybridity, overcoming city pressure without losing sight of the excitement and pleasure that this pressure can provoke.

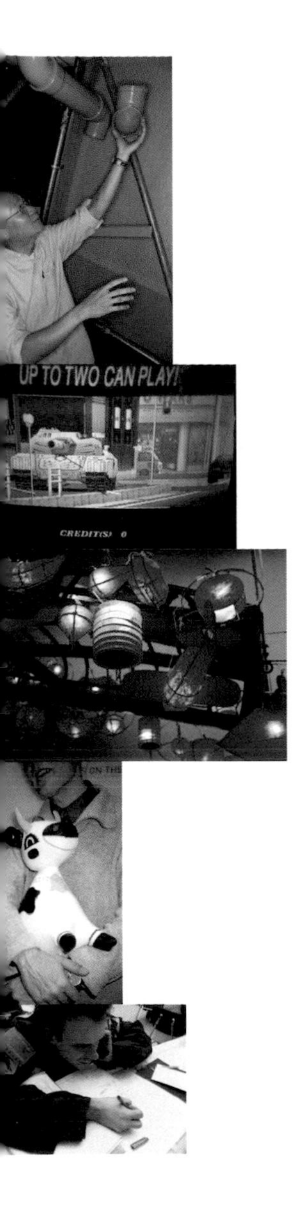

Ti-Nan Chi's *Z House*, Yung Ho Chang's miniature city within a building, Aaron Tan and Louise Low's studies of the Walled City, Sohn-Joo Minn's project for Seoul and the work of Kazuyo Seijima use the limitations of East Asian modernization in a simultaneous critique and celebration, looking within Asia for inspiration, rather than seeking conceptual guidance from Europe. Their projects tend to deal with the pressure of urban density by making 'urban infills' or interventions to improve existing conditions rather than larger operations aimed at creating a *tabula rasa*. This strategy suggests a significant change of direction in Asian urban development.

Artists are among the most active in the reconsideration of social structure and order necessitated by the conflicting demands of modernization and tradition. Many artists from different countries and cities (Chen Zhen, Cai Guo-Qiang, Zhang Peili, Geng Jianyi, Shen Yuan, Zheng Guogu, Wang Du, Zhou Tiehai and the Big Tail Elephant's Group – Lin Yilin, Xu Tan, Chen Shaoxiong and Liang Juhui – from China; Huang Chin-ho from Taiwan; Lee Bul and Choi Jeong Hwa from Korea; Arahmaiani from Indonesia; Oscar Ho from Hong Kong; Liew Kung Yu from Malaysia; Manit Sriwanichpoom from Thailand...) are making work which deals critically, and often ironically and humorously, with the conflict between consumer society and human existence and the schizophrenic frenzy of the new Asian urban condition. Chen Zhen's *Precipitous Parturition*, for example, imagines the consequence of China's stated ambition to upgrade all of the country's bicycles to cars, symbols of Western aspiration and achievement. Wang Du's *International Landscape* brings statues of Western prostitutes into Asian cityscapes as part of what he terms the 'landscape of the Other'. In Lee Bul's *Hydra*, on the other hand, it is the Eastern woman who is monumentalized and memorialized – as a huge blow up doll, a toy for the onlooker to play with.

Other artists, in search of a space for action within the cramped confines of the city, invent their own spaces and channels for expression in the very heart of the urban space. Like young architects, they work with the density of the megalopolis in order both to surmount and celebrate it. Like urban guerrillas, these artists (Navin Rawanchaikul and Surasi Kusolwong from Thailand; Lin Yilin, Zhan Wang, Yin Xiuzhen, Shi Yong and Tsang Tsou-choi from China; Yutaka Sone and Tsuyoshi Ozawa from Japan; Judy Freya Sibayan from the Philippines...) transform streets and construction sites into their own action ground, performing street actions which disturb the 'normal' order and rhythm of urban life, and finding new physical and conceptual space for art. Navin Rawanchaikul shows art in taxis, exploiting the legendary Bangkok traffic jams to capture the attention of his audience. Tsuyoshi Ozawa's *Nasubi Galleries* are similarly flexible and migratory – small boxes of the type used to hold milk bottles outside a house, which Ozawa offers to artists from all over the world as temporary and portable spaces for art. These artists explore the forgotten zones of the city, reanimating the urban void in a formidable bid for freedom and freshness amidst the density and intensity of urban life.

Another aspect of urban change in Asia is the Asian diaspora in the West. The globalization of the Asian economy and culture makes Asia increasingly open to the West, and to new forms of cultural hybridity and negotiation. Asian artists living abroad, such as Huang Yong Ping, Chen Zhen, Cai Guo-Qiang, Shen Yuan, Wang Du, Ken Lum and Koo Jeong-A, bring their critical observation of Asian urban life to the 'internationalization' of Asian culture, their distant angle of witness making their work particularly pungent. Chen Zhen's dragon made of bicycle tyres and toy cars, a powerful expression of this special voice, was made in Denmark specifically for the exhibition *Cities on the Move.*

In the last two years, Asia has seen the most serious financial crisis in its post-war history – an economic meltdown. In consequence, some nations and cities are suffering renewed political, social and cultural instability, causing a knock-on effect on the whole global economy. Artists are reacting to the changing situation by advocating a reform of the political and financial strategies which were the real cause of the crisis – the 'bubble economy' seen as the fastest route towards modernization. The work of Andar Manik, Marintan Sirait and Heri Dono exposes the political conflicts in Indonesia. In his *Vitrine of Contemporary Events*, Wong Hoy Cheong urges active resistance to the degeneration of democracy in Malaysia. Viewers are invited to participate in the artist's struggles, signing and sending a petition, and contributing a thumbprint which becomes part of a *Tapestry of Justice.* Ryuji Miyamoto's photographs of Kobe after the earthquake of 1995 not only show the impact of natural disaster on the city, but also hint at the disastrous instability of the economic system which supported the city.

The effects of the economic crisis are by no means uniformly negative. On the contrary, more and more people living in East Asia are beginning to understand the necessity of reconsidering the success story of the Tiger economies and to invest in longer-sighted strategies of financial, political and social development. As for the urban future, the region's architects are debating how to change the model of modernization. Bangkok, for example, was the first city to be literally interrupted by the crisis. Skyscrapers were abruptly abandoned when developers found themselves short of money. Now, architects who lost their contracts in the crisis work to transform the half-built, empty skyscrapers into useful and humane city structures. Taking inspiration from the homeless living in constantly-changing cardboard houses, architects in Bangkok are developing a new, flexible, relevant and constantly changing language of urban architecture and art. There is an

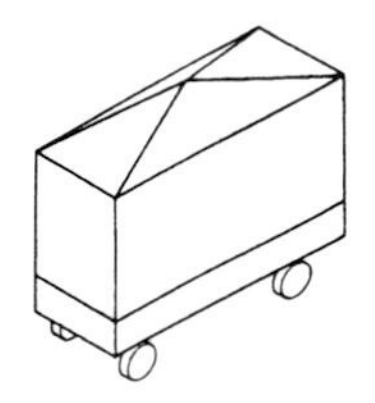
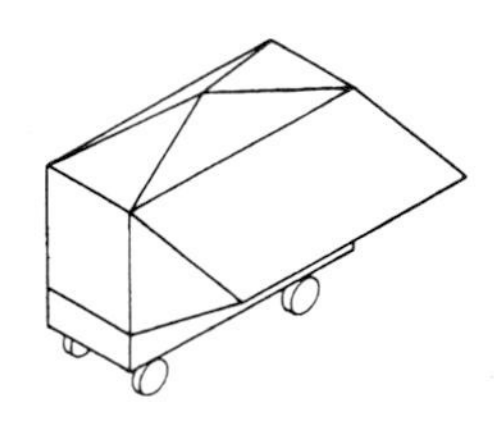
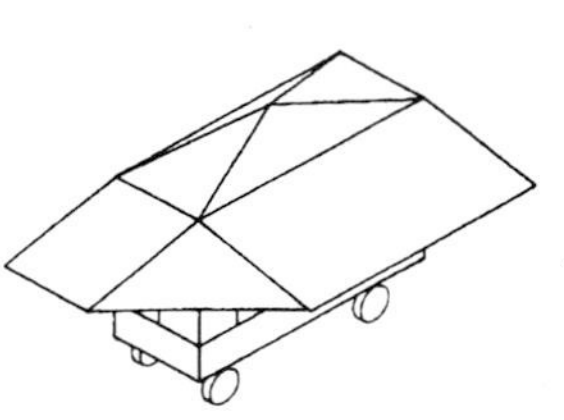
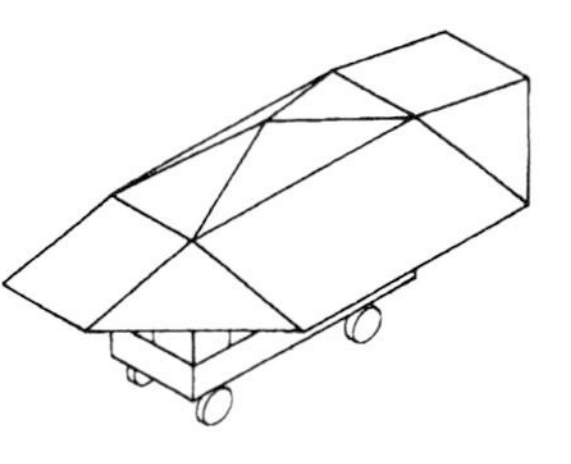

acknowledgement that urban space should be able to rebuild itself, to deal with the movement, change and mutation (including crisis) that is a condition of urban life.

Cities on the Move, as an exhibition, is one such ever-evolving 'event city'; constantly changing, reinventing, renovating, adapting itself to different venues and encouraging cross-disciplinary and trans-national collaboration. In London, it finds itself in one of the most substantial Asian communities in the West. Asian artists are playing an increasingly important part in the contemporary art scene. Many major Asian architects have studied, taught and worked in London, while London architects such as Norman Foster, Richard Rogers and Peter Cook have worked frequently in Asia. Rem Koolhaas, who is based part of the time in London, has designed the installation of the exhibition in the Hayward Gallery together with Ole Scheeren. Thinking the exhibition through conceptually and thematically, they have recycled elements from previous exhibition installations at the Hayward – most notably Zaha Hadid's designs for *Addressing the Century: 100 Years of Art & Fashion* and Robert Barnes' architecture for *Patrick Caulfield* – to make an exhibition design which is a complex, dynamic system based on use, a microcosm of the modern city.

Cities on the Move celebrates the contemporary East Asian urban condition as shifting, expanding, modernizing, unstable and exciting. An anecdote: Cedric Price – a respected architect whose reflections on urban conditions, together with his often very critical stance towards architecture, make him a hero for many young architects and artists in Asia and elsewhere – recently asked an equally respected architect a loaded question at the end of a lecture: 'How long do you want your building to last?' An answer had perhaps already been provided by the title of a lecture Toyo Ito gave at the time of the first showing of *Cities on the Move* in Vienna in 1997: 'Buildings die'.

Cedric Price
Demountable Market Stall, 1987

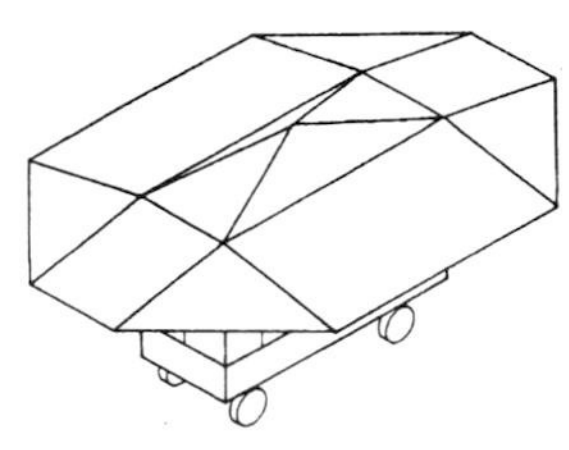

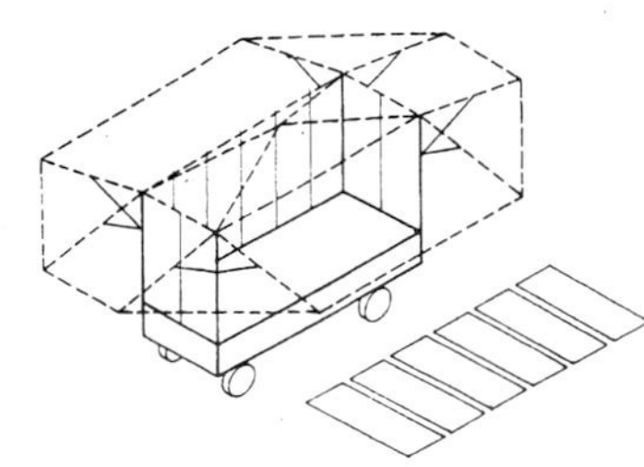

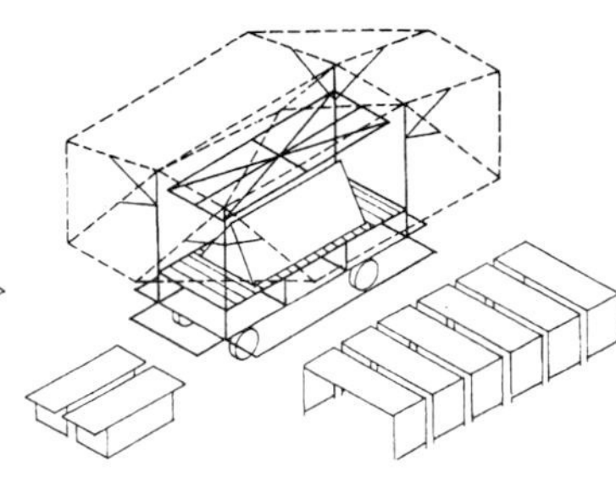

An Accelerated Merzbau

Rem Koolhaas, Exhibition Architect
Hans-Ulrich Obrist, Exhibition Co-curator

HUO: When first approached by the Hayward Gallery to make a design for the installation of *Cities on the Move*, your proposal was to recycle other architects' recent exhibition designs for the gallery rather than producing a single, unified scheme.

RK: I've always tried to be 'economical' with our imagination. Schwitters' Merzbau was an accumulation of (urban) debris that was reassembled a number of times. [From 1925, the German artist Kurt Schwitters made his Merzbau, which was declared 'unfinished, and on principle' when he was forced out of Germany in 1936.] Here, Ole Scheeren and I have tried first to accumulate previous Hayward designs, then to reassemble them, almost as a form of urbanism. I thought it would be nice if the show revealed a number of things about the Hayward, especially since the existence of this very building is currently under question.

HUO: You moved to London the year the Hayward opened, in 1968.

RK: Yes, lured by people like Peter Cook and Cedric Price and the thought of the architectural scene in London as some kind of huge club.

HUO: Do you remember the opening of the Hayward?

RK: Yes, of course. I mean it was THE event, and now I've lived here through all its declines and falls and resurrections. I think it's an incredibly vital and generous space, mainly because it has never conformed to anyone's expectation or model of what an exhibition space should be. Although everyone always complains about it, I think the Hayward has had some of the best and most extreme exhibitions that I've ever seen.

HUO: In the Louisiana Museum of Modern Art in Denmark, where the exhibition was immediately before coming to the Hayward, we organised the show into a number of different typologies of cities, following the many many interconnected spaces of the building's architecture. You decided not to do that at the Hayward.

RK: I was worried about dispersal. The Hayward doesn't have sufficient different areas to divide the exhibition into many city typologies, and I wanted certain main points to be evident. I thought we should see whether we could compress the show into four or five cities, with a sense of introduction and some kind of compression chamber that tells you you're about to enter a continent in total upheaval and turmoil.

So, in the light of the recycling of previous Hayward exhibitions' architecture, what we have done is keep the basic structure from the previous *Patrick Caulfield* exhibition, and add many of the objects that Zaha Hadid designed for *Addressing the Century: 100 Years of Art & Fashion* before that. We use the same circuit as for the *Caulfield*, but we modify it, so that when you enter, there is a big arrow telling you which way to go, but there is also a smaller passage which goes to the red light district. We'll do newness, like airport construction, but we'll also do decay, sex and drugs like in a real city.

HUO: You think that at present the exhibition is not sexual enough?

RK: Yes, very unsexual. I mean, given the fact that there is an enormous volume of sex tourism and that sex is one of the most important forms of transaction between people in cities, this show as it has been so far is almost oblivious to it. The problem is doing it without exoticism, and it's always difficult because of this reticence in Asia to talk about it. This I think is actually a really critical thing...

HUO: And the architects?

RK: It is a difficult issue for architects, how to deal with such an explosive phenomenon that seems to flourish beyond individual architects. How to connect to it? We'll put all the architecture together, into a sterile room of architecture...

HUO: A torture chamber of architecture?

RK: It's where my projects will go too...

HUO: So there is no value judgement?

RK: No, no value judgement, and I think this will let the works contaminate each other in an interesting way.

Above and opposite: Rem Koolhaas and Ole Scheeren, design for *Urbanpaper*, 1999 Images: Harvard Design School Project on the City, © the artists Overleaf: design for *Cities on the Move* at the Hayward Gallery, London. Work in progress

HUO: Will there be other changes to the *Caulfield* architecture on the ground floor?

RK: We'll make a kind of intimate streetscape with Zaha Hadid's plinths, turning them into video buildings and vitrines for icons so that one room becomes some kind of monumental alley. We'll tunnel through the corridor surrounding the ramp and put in some videos and plaster the walls with Armin Linke's installation photographs. Overhead will be Chen Zhen's bicycle/car dragon.

HUO: Let's move to the top floor.

RK: It will be a 'commercial area' – projectors in the staircase, and we'll use another of Zaha's big vitrines to create a cinema. Then we'll have an area with things for sale which will make us see the nearby cinema as commercial too. And then the space will end in political protest where eggs are thrown.

HUO: You mentioned the idea of urban wallpaper.

RK: The walls of the whole ground floor should be covered with wallpaper; wallpaper of urban images, of urban realities. There will be no words, with the exception of occasionally the front page of a newspaper. The wallpaper is a background, a grey presence everywhere, kind of overwhelming. That's the whole point of cities, a nightmare in a way. An overkill. Urban overkill inside the Hayward.

BUDDAH

STREET

● PHOTO OPPORTUNITY

AIRPORTS

ARCHITECTURE

NEWNESS

BLANDNESS

STERILITY

POL

DECAY

DANGER

● PHOTO OPPORTUNITY

MESS

● PHOTO OPPORTUNITY

SEX

FOOD

DRUGS

● PHOTO OPPORTUNITY

TICS

COMMERCIAL ZONE

CINEMA

Cities on the Move
Works and Biographies

Arahmaiani

Artist born in 1961 in Bandung, Indonesia. Lives and works in Bandung and Bangkok.
Exhibitions include: VI Biennial de la Havana, Cuba 1997; Current Art in South East Asia: White Cases, Museum of Contemporary Art, Tokyo and Hiroshima 1997; Traditions/Tensions, Asia Society Gallery, New York 1996; Asia-Pacific Triennial, Brisbane 1996.

Handle without Care, 1996–97
Single screen video, running time 12 minutes

Paul ANDREU

Architect born in 1938 in Caudéron, France. Lives and works in Paris.
Trained as an Engineer at the Ecole Polytechnique de France (1961), a Civil Engineer at the Ecole Nationale des Ponts et Chausseés, France (1963) and an Architect at the Ecole Nationale Supérieure des Beaux-Arts, France (1968). Director of Architecture and Engineering, Aeroports de Paris. Specialist in airport architecture – work includes: Jakarta, Dar es Salaam, Cairo, Brunei, Nice Côte d'Azur, Bordeaux, Point à Pitre and Shanghai-Pudong.
Projects include: French Terminal, Channel Tunnel; Guangzhou New Stadium 1996; New Shanghai International Airport 1996; CDG Airport, Terminal 2F, Paris 1996; Master Plan and Urbanism, Avenue Nouvelle, Paris 1996; Osaka Maritime Museum, Japan 1995; Ski-jump runway, Winter Olympic Games 1992; Master Plan Review, Preliminary Design – Manila International Airport 1990.

Guangzhou New Baiyun International Airport, 1998
Model and drawings

Nobuyoshi ARAKI

Artist born in 1940 in Tokyo, Japan. Lives and works in Tokyo.
Solo exhibitions include: Araki Retrographs, Hara Museum, Tokyo 1997; Flower Compositions, JM Gallery, Tokyo 1997; A's Life, La For't Harajuku, Tokyo 1997; Secession, Vienna 1997; From Close Range, Blum & Poe, Los Angeles 1996.
Group exhibitions include: Amours, Fondation Cartier pour l'art contemporain, 1997; The Dead, National Museum of Photography, Film and Television, Horsens Museum, Denmark 1996; Portrait of a Woman, Shoutou Museum, Tokyo 1996.

Hong Kong Kiss, 1997
CD-Rom

Untitled, 1997
Photographs of Taipei and Bangkok

Shigeru BAN

Architect born in 1957 in Tokyo. Lives and works in Tokyo.
Studied at Southern California Institute of Architecture (1977–80) and Cooper Union School of Architecture (1980–82). Established practice in Tokyo in 1985. Recent works include: Furniture House #3, Kanagawa 1998; Ivy Structure House, Tokyo 1998; Issey Miyake Paris Collection stage set design, Paris 1998; Paper Stage Design, Kabukiza Theatre, Tokyo 1997; Paper Log House – Paper Tube Structure #7, Kobe, Hyogo 1995.
Recent exhibitions and awards include: Tohoku Prize, Architectural Institute of Japan 1998; GIA prize for the best young architect of the year 1997; Innovative Award, Tokyo Journal 1996; Paper Church and Volunteers at Kobe, Kenchikuka Club 1996.

Paper Log House, 1999
Site-specific house made from cardboard tubes and beer crates

Duangrit BUNNAG

Architect born in 1966 in Bangkok, Thailand. Lives and works in Thailand.
Studied at Chualongkorn University, Bangkok (B.Arch. (Hon.), 1989). Worked as an architect in a design firm for 5 years. Studied at the Architectural Association School of Architecture, London (1993-94, Graduate Diploma 1995). Senior Architect at ARCHITECTS 49; editor of *art4d*, an architecture, design and art monthly magazine; lecturer and critic.

Art4d
Magazines

CAI Guo-Qiang

Artist born in 1957 in Quanzhou, China. Lives and works in New York.
Solo exhibitions include: Flying Dragon in the Heavens, Louisiana Museum of Modern Art, Denmark 1997; Cultural Melting Bath: Projects for the 20th Century, Queens Museum of Art, New York 1997. Group exhibitions include: Future, Past, Present: 47th Venice Biennale, Italy 1997; Performance Anxiety, Museum of Contemporary Art, Chicago and San Diego, SITE, Santa Fe 1997

Red Golf, 1997–99
Site-specific golf course installation

Red Golf, 1997-99, as shown at Louisiana Museum of Modern Art

Yung Ho CHANG

© the artist 1999

Architect born in 1956 in Beijing, China. Lives and works in Beijing.
After studying and teaching in the USA, founded the Atelier Feichang Jianzhu with Lu Lija in Beijing in 1993. Recent research focuses on the discussion of urban change in Beijing in a global context.
Prizes and exhibitions include: Innovation Architecture in Asia, Osaka 1996; Progress Architecture Award Exhibition, San Francisco 1996.

The Snake Legs, 1999, as shown at Louisiana Museum of Modern Art

The Snake Legs, 1999
Architectural solution for Cities on the Move at the Louisiana Museum of Modern Art

CHEN Shaoxiong

Artist born in Shantou, China. Lives and works in Guangzhou.
Exhibitions include: Demonstration of Video Art '97 China, Beijing 1997; Another Long March – Chinese Conceptual Art 1997, Fundament Foundation, Chasse Kazerne, Breda, The Netherlands 1997; Phenomenon and Image in Video Art, China Fine Art Academy, Hangzhou 1996; In the Name of Art, The Art Museum of Liu Haishu, Shanghai 1996; Possibility, Zhong Guang Building, Guangzhou 1996.

Untitled, 1997; Street I, II & III, 1998
Video installation in gallery toilets; street models

©Chen Zhen 1999

CHEN Zhen

Artist born in Shanghai, China. Lives and works in Paris, Shanghai and New York.
Solo exhibitions include: Fu Dao/Fu Dao, Upside-Down Buddha/Arrival at Good Fortune, CCA, Kitakyushu, Japan 1997; Daily Incantation, Deitch Projects, New York 1996.
Group exhibitions include: Hong Kong etc, 2nd Johannesburg Biennale, South Africa 1997; Hybrid, Kwangju Biennale, Korea 1997; L'Autre, Lyon Biennial, Maison de Lyon, France 1997.
www. shanghart.com/chenzhen/index

Precipitous Parturition, 1999
Installation with bicycle inner tubes, toy cars and bicycles

Precipitous Parturition, 1999 (detail), as shown at Louisiana Museum of Modern Art

CHI Ti-Nan

Architect born in 1959 in Taipei, Taiwan. Lives and works in Taipei.
Selected exhibitions: Tangibleintangible, solo exhibition, IT Park September 1998; Possibly big possibly small, group exhibition, Architectural Association, London 1998.

Connection, 1997
Computer image of Hong Kong

CHOI Jeong Hwa

Artist born in 1961 in Seoul, Korea. Lives and works in Seoul.
Exhibitions include: Fast Forward, Power Plant Museum, Toronto, Canada 1997; OZ Gallery, Paris, France 1997; Centre of Academic Resources, Chulalongkorn University, Bangkok 1997; Promenade in Asia, Shiseido Gallery, Tokyo, Japan 1997; Technology & Antitechnology, Art & Culture Centre, Seoul 1996; Youthful Trend – The Planning Exhibition, Jun-Ju Museum, Jun-Ju 1996.

Fast Forward, 1997
Video, running time 2 minutes

Heri DONO

Artist born in 1960 in Jakarta, Indonesia. Lives and works in Yogyakarta.
Exhibitions include: Exploring the Future of the Imagination, The Inter Communication Centre Tokyo, Japan 1997; Universalis, 23rd Biennial International São Paulo, Brazil 1996; Traditions/Tensions – Contemporary Art in Asia, The Asia Society, New York 1996; Jurassic Technologies, 10th Biennial of Sydney 1996; Beyond the Border. 1st Kwangju Biennial, Korea.

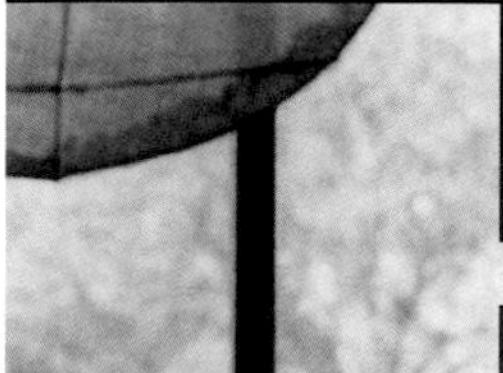

Inner City, 1997; Inner City, 1999
Multi-media installation with 15 fibreglass angels fitted with sound devices transmitting bird and insect song and radio interference; mannequin with slide and video projections

EDGE

Architecture practice established in 1994 in Hong Kong by Gary Chang and Michael Chan.
Michael Chan born in 1967 in Hong Kong. Studied at Hong Kong University (BA Architectural Studies 1989, BA Architecture 1993). From 1993, a member of the Hong Kong Institute of Architects; from 1997, Visiting Design Lecturer at the Faculty of Architecture, Hong Kong University.
Gary Chang born in Hong Kong in 1962. Studied at Hong Kong University (BA Architectural Studies 1985, BA Architecture 1987). Lecturer in Design (part time) in the faculty of Architecture, Hong Kong University, since 1995.
EDGE projects include: Broadway Cinematheque, Market Republic Grocery Market, Office of Post Production Sound and Digital Vision Ltd.

Sand Pile City, Hong Kong, 1997
Architectural plans

FOREIGN OFFICE

Architectural practice based in London since 1995. Directors: Farshid Moussavi and Alejandro Zaera-Polo.
Farshid Moussavi: British, born 1965. Trained at Dundee University, Scotland (B.Sc.Arch.), The Bartlett School of Architecture (Dipl.Arch.) and Harvard University Graduate School of Design (MARCHII). Design Visiting Professor at the Berlage Postgraduate Architecture Institute, Amsterdam, and Unit Master at the Architectural Association School of Architecture, London.
Alejandro Zaera-Polo: Spanish, born 1963. Trained at E.T.S. of Architecture in Madrid and Harvard University Graduate School of Design (MARCHII). Lecturer at Princeton University, New York, and Visiting Critic at the Berlage Postgraduate Architecture Institute, Amsterdam.
Recent projects include: New Belgo Restaurants in London 1999, Bristol 1998 and New York 1998; Bermondsey Antiques Market Design Commission 1997; Mirage City – Urban design ideas study commission for a new island near Main Land China 1997; Yokohama International Ferry Terminal, Japan, ongoing.

Yokohama International Ferry Terminal, 1996–98
Model, drawings and computer animation

Anne FRÉMY

Artist born in 1955. Lives and works in Paris.
Work takes the form of found images, series and ensembles, photographs and films of cities, extreme architectural conditions, utopias and dystopias, micro-climates, communities, the relationship between the urban and the natural, water, cities as natural spaces...
Work includes: Isola, Galerie de L'Ecole des Beaux-Arts de Quimper, France 1999; Laureate of the programme, 'L'Envers des Villes', AFAA-Caisse des Dépots et Consignations, Tokyo, Reykjavik 1998; Vertigo, le Magasin, Grenoble, France 1998; L'Heure Universelle, Editions Art 3, Valence 1998; Architecture(s) archives, Edition Purple Books, Paris 1997; Modell, Programme Containerize, Berlin 1997.

Tokyo Marine, 1999
Video projection, running time 10 minutes

opposite:
Heri Dono, Inner City, 1997, as shown at Louisiana Museum of Modern Art
right:
Still from Anne Frémy, Tokyo Marine, 1999

GENG Jianyi

Artist born in 1962 in Zhengzhou, China. Lives and works in Hangzhou.
Exhibitions include: Immutability and Fashion: Chinese Contemporary Art in the Midst of Changing Surroundings, Kirin Art Space Harajuku, Tokyo Plaza, Osaka, Altium, Fukuoka, Japan 1997; Another Long March: Chinese Conceptual Art 1997, Breda, The Netherlands 1997; China-Aktuelles aus 15 Ateliers, Performances Installationen, Munich, Germany 1996; Image and Phenomena, Gallery of China Academy of Fine Arts, Hangzhou 1996.

Reasonable Relationship
Text panels and photographs

Simryn GILL

Artist born in 1959 in Singapore. Lives and works in Port Dickson, Malaysia.
Interested in the issues of migration, transnational dislocation and the cultural and political impulses of post-colonialism. Recent work also deals with politics of textual production.
Exhibitions include: The Art Gallery of New South Wales, 1997; Naoshima Contemporary Art Museum, Japan 1995, 46th Venice Biennale, Italy 1995; National Art Gallery, Malaysia 1994.

Interlopers, 1997–99
Postal project with stamps made by the artist

Dominique GONZALEZ-FOERSTER

Artist born in 1965 in Strasbourg. Lives and works in Paris.
Solo exhibitions include: Tropicale Modernite (with Jens Hoffmann), Pavilion Mies van der Rohe, Barcelona 1999; Pavillon d'Argent, Galerie Mot & Van Den Boogaard, Brussels 1999; Interiorisme, Galerie Jennifer Flay, Paris 1999; Home Cinema, Robert Prime, London 1998; ARC – Musée d'Art Moderne de la Ville de Paris 1998; Fille/Garçon, Gallery Koyanagi, Tokyo 1995; Interieures, Stedelijk Museum, Amsterdam 1994; The Daughter of a Taoist, Esther Schipper, Cologne 1991.
Group exhibitions include: Berlin Biennale 1998; Premises... Guggenheim Museum Soho, New York 1998; Urban Mirage, Art Document 097, Hiroshima 1997; Auto-Reverse, Magasin Grenoble 1996; The Winter of Love, PS1, New York 1994.

Mini-Festival Building, 1999
Presentation of videos by emerging Asian and European artists, journalists and film makers. Collaborating artists: Olivier Bardin, Laetitia Benat, Hsia-Fei Chang, Hu Chin-Fong, Gill Gonzalez-Foerster, Kim Sup, Go Watanabe, Mimi Wong, Delphine Zampetti

HANAYO

Performer currently based in London.
Began education as a junior geisha in 1989. In 1991, published her first book, *Oshakuchan No 1* about her life in the geisha world. In 1992, formed a new band, *Muscats*, with Massami Akita from *Merzbow* and Masaya Nakahara from *Violent Onsen Geisha*. In 1995, finished her work as a geisha and moved to Europe, where she formed the band *Vapid Dolly* with Dizzy Q Viper (ex *Daisy Chainsaw*). In 1997, she formed the band *Blisters*, with the Sultans in London, and performed a theatre-play (directed by Christoph Schlingensief) at Documenta X, Hybrid Workspace, Kassel, Germany 1997.

Untitled, 1998
Photographs

HARVARD PROJECT

Rem Koolhaas, Tae Wook Cha, Nicole Natalie Gaenzler, Jutki Gunter, Daniel Herman, Hiromi Hosoya, Jeffrey Inaba, Srdjan Jovanovic Weiss, Sze Tsung Leong, Teng-Wui Leong, Kiwa Matsushita, John Mc Morrough, Juan Palop-Casado, Markus Schaefer, tran Vinh, Louise Wyman.
The Harvard Design School Project on the City, unofficially known as 'The Project for what used to be called the City' researches the effects of modernization on the urban consciousness. The focus of its second iteration is 'shopping' – a field relatively invisible to the so-called 'official' architectural and urban professions, with its own internal logic, language and velocities.

Shopping, 1997
Prints

Itsuko HASEGAWA

Architect born in 1941 in Shizuoka, Japan. Lives and works in Tokyo.
Established the Itsuko Hasegawa Atelier in 1979. Elected an Honorary Fellow of the RIBA in 1997.
Awards received include: the Design Prize from the Architectural institute of Japan for her Bizan Hall project, 1986; Japanese Cultural Design Award for her residential projects; first prize in the official competition for the Shonandai Cultural Centre. Currently working on her winning entry for the Niigata City Performing Arts Centre and Area Development.

Niigata City Performing Arts Centre, 1993–98; Yokohama International Port Terminal, 1994
Model and plans; model

David d'HEILLY & Kayoko OTA

David d'Heilly is a writer and film maker based in Tokyo. Founder and Principle of 2dk Co., Ltd.
Kayoko Ota is a writer based in Tokyo. Editor/Producer of 2dk Co., Ltd.; co-founder of the Workshop for Architecture and Urbanism, and former publisher of the independent bilingual magazine TELESCOPE.

You are Here, 1997–99; Happy Paranoia, 1999
Site specific multi-media installation of road construction site with projection and sound; bookshop installation of East Asian books and periodicals

David d'Heilly & Kayoko Ota, You are Here, 1997–99, as shown at Louisiana Museum of Modern Art

Jacques HERZOG & Pierre DE MEURON

Architecture practice founded in Basel, Switzerland in 1978 by Jacques Herzog and Pierre de Meuron. Four partners:
Jacques Herzog, born in 1950 in Basel, Switzerland. Studied at the ETH Zurich, 1975. Visiting professor at Harvard University, Cambridge, Mass., USA, 1996–98.
Pierre de Meuron, born in 1950 in Basel, Switzerland. Studied at the ETH Zurich, 1975. Visiting professor at Harvard University, Cambridge, Mass., USA.
Harry Gugger, born in 1956 in Grenzenbach, Switzerland. Studied at the ETH Zurich, 1990. Partnership with Herzog & de Meuron 1991. Visiting Professor at the Hochschule für Architektur und Bauwesen, Weimar, Germany, 1994.
Christine Binswanger, born in 1964 in Kreuzlingen, Switzerland. Studied at the ETH Zurich, 1990. Collaboration with Herzog & de Meuron 1991, partnership 1994.

Once upon a Time there was a City, 1996
Video, running time 8 minutes 30 seconds
with René Pulfer

回天之術
竹園有個女
人佢老公
大概三年前
咁就回天之術，真係天意

Oscar HO

Artist born in 1956 in Hong Kong. Lives and works in Hong Kong.
Exhibition Director of the Hong Kong Arts Centre since 1988.
Exhibitions include: Recognising with the Past, European touring exhibition 1996-97; Hong Kong Now, US touring exhibition 1997-98; Vibrancy, Hong Kong Museum of Art, Hong Kong 1992; The Art of Assemblage, Art Gallery, Union Building, University of California, USA 1998.

Stories around Town, 1992-97
City drawings

Richard HO

Architect born in 1956 in Singapore. Lives and works in Singapore.
Studied at the National University of Singapore (graduated 1982). Established Richard Ho Architects in 1991. The firm believes in using architecture as an expression of the continuity of the history of civilization, the memory of cities and man's unending endeavour to be in harmony with his soul and the world in which he lives. This necessarily rejects any notion of architectural fashion or exhibitionism or architecture-for-architecture's sake.

Memory & Analogy, 1996
Architectural plan

Tao HO

Architect, urban designer and artist born in 1936 in Shanghai, China.
Studied at Williams College (BA in Art History, Theology and Music) and Harvard University (MA in Architecture). Worked as a personal assistant to Walter Gropius. TAOHO Design has been based in Hong Kong since 1968, with many projects in China. In 1997, won the Crystal Award of the World Economic Forum in recognition of his achievements in bridging Eastern and Western culture through his architecture and art.

City Projects, 1983–97
Photographs and plans

opposite:
Oscar Ho, No resurrection, 1997, from Stories around Town

Takashi Homma,
print from Tokyo Suburbia

Takashi HOMMA

Artist born in 1962 in Tokyo, Japan. Lives and works in Tokyo.
Solo exhibitions include: Hyperballad, ASMUNDARSALUR, Reykjavik 1997; Sleep, Taka Ishii Gallery, Tokyo 1996; Baby Land, PARCO Gallery, Tokyo 1995.
Published works include: Hyperballad: Icelandscape Photography, Switch, Tokyo 1997; Switch, Cutie, Smart, Hanatsubaki, IDEA, H, S&M Sniper, Tokyo 1996; purple fashion, Paris 1996; I-D, London 1996; Ray Gun, Los Angeles.

Tokyo Suburbia
Prints and artist's book

HUANG Chin-ho

Artist born in 1956 in Chiayi, Taiwan. Lives and works in Taichung.
Solo exhibitions include: Railroad No. 15, Taichung 1993; Mu Shih Yuan Art Gallery, Taipei 1991.
Group exhibitions include: Art Taiwan, Museum of Contemporary Art, Sydney, Australia 1995; Localities of Desire, Museum of Contemporary Art, Sydney, Australia 1994; Taiwan Art, 1945–93, Taipei Fine Arts Museum 1993.

Fire, 1998; Jerusalem, 1998
Poster; slides

HUANG Yong Ping

Artist born in 1954 in Fujian, China. Has lived and worked in Paris since 1989.
One of the leading figures in the Chinese avant-garde movement which came to prominence in the 1980s. Leader of the group 'Xiamen Dada'.
Solo exhibitions include: De Appel Foundation, Amsterdam 1997; Fondation Cartier 1996.
Group exhibitions include: Hong Kong etc, Johannesburg Biennial 1997; Kwangju Biennial 1997; Sculpture Project, Münster 1997; Parisien(ne)s, London 1997; Face ‡ l'histoire, Paris 1996.

Turtle Town, 1997
Site specific installation with 52 plaster turtles, made for the Vienna Secession and adapted by architect Yung Ho Chang

Arata ISOZAKI

Architect born in 1931 in Oita City, Japan. Lives and works in Tokyo.
Founded Arata Isozaki and Associates in 1963.
Main works include: The Museum of Contemporary Art, Los Angeles 1981-86; Art Tower Mito 1986-90; Team Disney Building 1987-90; The Centre of Japanese Art and Technology, Krakow 1990-99; Nagi Museum of Contemporary Art 1991-94; Kyoto Concert Hall 1991-95; DOMUS: la Casa del hombre, la Corufa, Spain 1993-95; Project Haishi/Kaishi 1995 - .

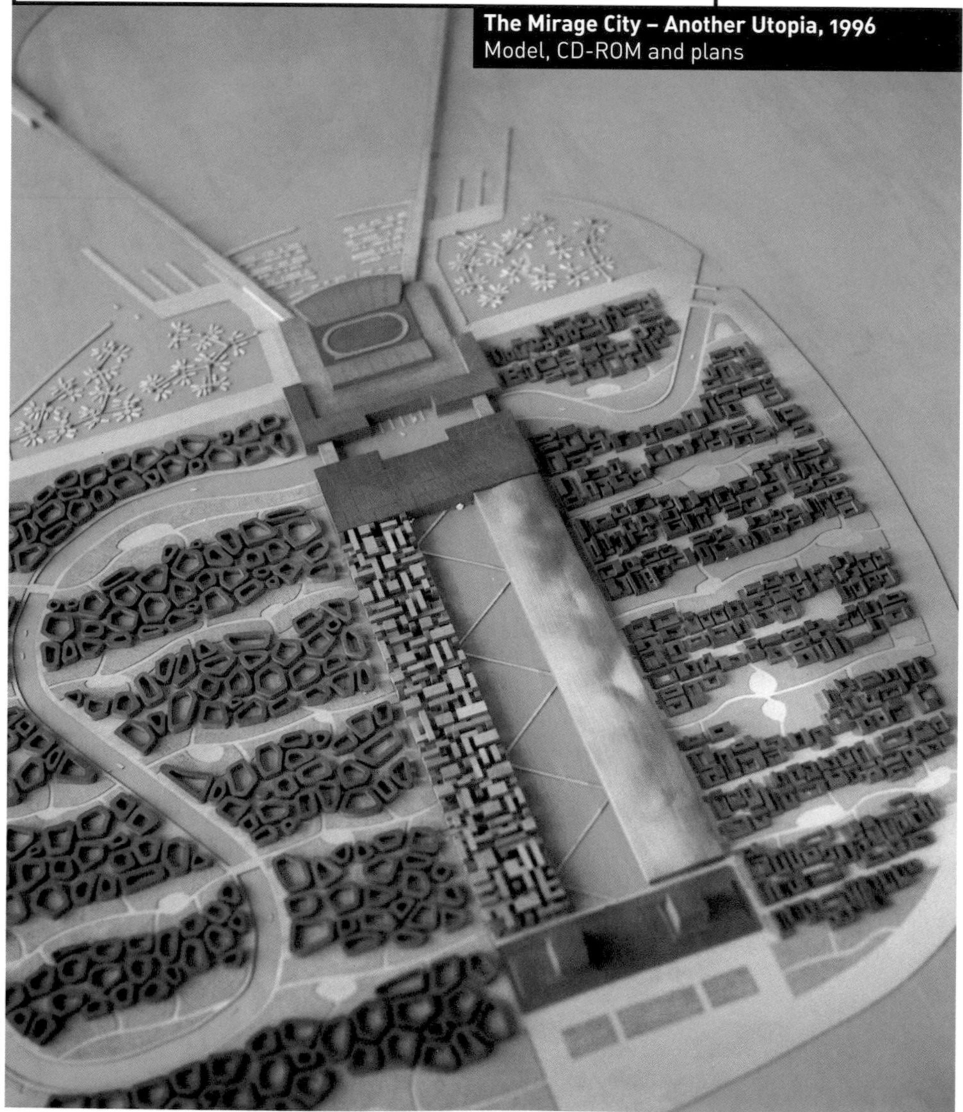

The Mirage City – Another Utopia, 1996
Model, CD-ROM and plans

Toyo ITO & Associates

Architect born in 1941 in Japan. Lives and works in Tokyo.
Studied at Tokyo University, Department of Architecture (graduated 1965). Established his own studio in 1971. Honorary Professor of Architecture, University of North London.
Works include: Yatsushiro Municipal Museum; Shimosuwa Municipal Museum, Fire Station, Yatsushiro; L-Hall, Nagaoka; O-Domge, Odate.

Garden of Microchips, 1998
Installation with cityscapes and ultra violet light

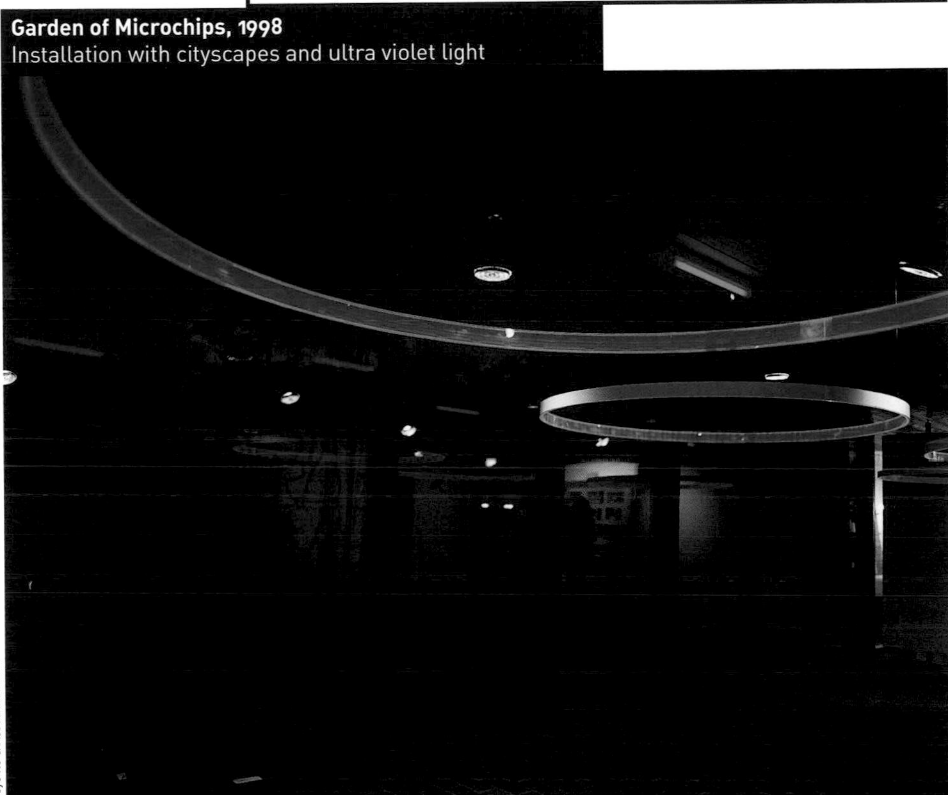

Garden of Microchips, 1998, as shown at Louisiana Museum of Modern Art

Lucas JODOGNE

Artist living and working in Belgium.

Punggol Road Looking towards Hougang; Mjd Darul Makmur from BLK 225; Bishan Town from Jalan Penimpin Industrial Building
Photographs

Sumet JUMSAI

Architect born in 1939 in Bangkok, Thailand. Lives and works in Bangkok.
Studied architecture at Cambridge University (PhD, 1958-67).
Chairman of Bangkok-based architectural firm SJA 3D Co. Ltd. In private practice since 1969, responsible for over 200 projects.
Academic activities: fellow of the Royal Society of Arts (FRSA), UK; Faculty member of the Department of Architecture, Cambridge University since 1991.
Politics and social work: member of Thai government and NGO committees on the environment, historic conservation, art & culture, urban development and slum community work.
Recent work: new UN-related institute in Geneva, awarded through international competition.

Shapes on the Move – Concept for a (or any) building, 1997
3 photographic panels

Chitti Kasemkitvatana, Neeeooon, 1997-99, as shown at Louisiana Museum of Modern Art

Chitti KASEMKITVATANA

Artist born in 1969 in Bangkok, Thailand. Lives and works in Bangkok.
Solo exhibitions include: When 2 be come 1, About Café, Bangkok 1996.
Group exhibitions include: Hidden Agenda, Project 304, Bangkok 1996; Do It-Thai Version, Bangkok University Art Gallery, Bangkok 1996.

Neeeooon, 1997-99
Site-specific light installation

KAY Ngee Tan

Born in 1956 in Singapore. Trained at the National University of Singapore and the Architectural Association, London. Worked for Arup Associates, London 1984–90. Set up KNTA London in 1990, and KNTA Singapore (with Teck Kiam Tan) in 1993. Lives and works in London and Singapore.

Borderline, 1998
Installation with revolving projections

KHOO Eric

Film maker born in 1965 in Singapore. Lives and works in London.
Studied at the City Art Institute in Sydney (BA, 1995).
Works include: *Barbie Digs Joe*; *August*; *New Rock School* (with Nazir Husain); *The Punk Rocker And...*; *Symphony 92.4FM*; *Pain*; *Mee Pok Man.*
International festivals in which his work has been shown include: Toronto; Hong Kong; San Francisco.

12 Storeys, 1997
Film, running time 45 minutes

Kay Ngee Tan, Borderline, 1998, as shown at the Louisiana Museum of Modern Art

Kiyonori KIKUTAKE

Architect born in 1928 in Japan. Lives and works in Tokyo.
In 1958, the first to propose a Marine City Project, and has been working on Floating System projects ever since. In 1960, he proposed the concept of a metabolic architecture which integrates tradition with modernity, as in his Sky House and Izumo Shrine. For housing, he has pursued the realisation of marine cities, super high-rise housing and mega structures, integrating environmental considerations for sustainable development.

Okinawa Ocean Expo, 1975
Aquapolis, 1975
Panels; photographs

Jinai KIM

Architect and planner living and working in Seoul.
Director of the SEOUL FORUM Inc. and of ARCHFORUM, an internet journal of architecture and urbanism.
Urban design work includes: Pusan Teleport Town; Micro-Electronic Multiples; Geo-City; Sanbon New Town.
Author of 17 books including: Seoulness; House wish for the 21st Century; Splendid China.
www.archforum.com/special/shangtse

Space Intervention in Time; the Age of City Culture 1990-2001
Installation with painting, calendars and collages

Soo-Ja KIM

Artist born in 1957 in Taegu, Korea. Lives and works in Seoul.
Solo exhibitions include: A Laundry Field/Sewing into Walking, MAGASIN, Centre national d'art contemporain de Grenoble 1997.
Group exhibitions include: De-Genderism, Setagaya Art Museum, Tokyo 1997; Tradition/Tensions, touring exhibition Vancouver Art Gallery, The Asia Society, New York 1997; The 5th Istanbul Biennial, Istanbul 1997.

Cities on the Move – 2727 km Bottari Truck, 1997; Seoul Subway Sound, 1997
Video; sound recording

Still from Cities on the Move – 2727 km Bottari Truck, 1997

KIM Yun-Tae

Artist born in 1962 in Unchoen, Korea. Lives and works in Seoul.
Exhibitions include: Kwangju Biennial, Korea 1997; Com-Art Show, Suwon, Korea 1995.
Film and video festivals include: Asian-Pacific Film Festival, Cheju, Korea 1997; Indie-Forum Film Festival, Seoul, Korea 1997; Vancouver International Film Festival, Canada 1997.

Concoction, Slapdash, 1996; Metro/Aquarium, 1997
Video compilation, running time 3 minutes

Takeshi KITANO (Beat Takeshi)

Film maker and performer born in 1947 in Tokyo, Japan. Lives and works in Tokyo.
Films directed include: *Kids Return*, 1996; *Minna Yattereuka (Getting Any?)*, 1995; *Sonatine*, 1993; *Ano Natsu, Ichiban Shizukana Uni (A Scene at the Sea)*, 1991.
Appears regularly in TV shows including: *Super Jockey*, NTV; *Sekai Maru Mie, TV Tokusobu (Around the World, TV Special Task Force)*, NTV; *Beat Takeshi no TV Tackle (Beat Takeshi's Tackle TV)*, TV Asahi.

Kids Return, 1996
Film, running time 104 minutes

Portrait of Takeshi Kitano on the set of Kids Return

Karl Heinz KLOPF

Artist born in 1956 in Linz, Austria. Lives and works in Vienna.
Exhibitions include: Trabant, Vienna 1997; Lust und Leere, Kunsthalle Vienna 1997; Splace, Gallery Stadtpark, Krens 1996; Check In/ Check Out, Za Mocca Foundation, Tokyo 1996; Vier Positionen für Raum, Galerie Lendl, Graz 1995; Platz, Gallery in the Stifterhaus, Linz 1994; Hotel, Culturcentrum Wolkenstein, Stainach 1993; Game Without Frontiers, Mucsarnok, Budapest 1993.

Environments, 1998
Video, running time 86 minutes

Still from Environments, 1998

Aglaia KONRAD

Artist born in 1960 in Salzburg. Lives and works in Brussels.
Solo exhibitions include: Galerie Fotomania, Rotterdam 1996; Galerie De Vaalserberg, Rotterdam 1995; Stedelijk Museum, Amsterdam 1995; Salzberger Kunstverein, Salzburg 1993.
Group exhibitions include: Documenta X, Kassel 1997; Groene Pasen, Durele 1997; Prospect 96, Frankfurt 1996; Antagonismes, Paris, Lausanne 1996.

Untitled, 1999
Site-specific photographic installation

KOO Jeong-A

Artist born in 1967 in Seoul, Korea. Lives and works everywhere.
Solo exhibitions include: Aquaduc, Musée d'art moderne de la ville de Paris 1997; too://www.so.up/there, 28 rue rousselet 75007 Paris 1997; Mousse a vos mesures, 16 rue etienne-marcel 75002 Paris 1995.
Group exhibitions include: Manifesta 1, Rotterdam 1996; Ducks Not On A Pond, Manchester 1995.

Snowy, Sunny Day, 1997–99
Site specific installation and photographs

Snowy, Sunny Day, 1997-99, as shown at capcMusée d'art contemporain de Bordeaux

Rem KOOLHAAS, OMA

Architect born in 1944 in Rotterdam, The Netherlands. Lives and works in Rotterdam and London.
Founded the Office for Metropolitan Architecture (OMA) with M Vriesendorp and E&Z Zenghelis in Rotterdam in 1975. Currently Professor of Architecture at Harvard University.
Books include: *Delirious New York, a Retroactive Manifesto for New York*, 1978; *S.M.L.XL.*, designed by Bruce Mau, 1995.
Buildings include: Netherlands Dance Theatre, The Hague; Nexus Housing, Fukuoka; Kunsthal, Rotterdam; Centre d'Affaires and Lille Grand Palais, Lille.

Hyperbuilding (Bangkok), 1997
Model, text and photographs

Model from Eco-Media-City, 1997

Kisho KUROKAWA

Architect born in 1934 in Nagaya, Japan. Studied Kyoto University, Department of Architecture, and Tokyo University, Graduate School of Architecture. One of the founders of the Metabolism Movement in 1960.
Major works include: National Ethnological Museum; National Bunraku Theatre; Nagoya City Art Museum; Hiroshima City Museum of Contemporary Aty; the Museum of Modern Art, Wakayama; the Japanese-German Centre, Berlin; the Chinese-Japanese Youth Centre, Beijing, China; Melbourne Centre, Australia; Pacific Tower, Paris, France.

Eco-Media-City, 1997; Kuala Lumpur Airport and Eco City
Model and drawing; slides, panels and book

Surasi KUSOLWONG

Artist born in 1965 in Ayutthaya, Thailand. Lives and works in Bangkok.

Solo exhibitions include: European Onishi Gallery, Nagoya, Japan 1988; Künstlerhaus Göttingen, Germany 1993; Die Brücke-Galerie, Stadt Braunschweig, Germany 1994; Kunstkreis Kloster Brunshausen, Bad Gandersheim, Germany 1994; Bangkok University Art Gallery, Bangkok, Thailand 1996.

Freedom of Choice (£1 each), 1999
Site-specific installation of a street market

You can take whatever you need, 1999, Louisiana Museum of Modern Art

LEE Bul

Artist born in 1964 in Yongwol, South Korea. Lives and works in Seoul, South Korea.
Solo exhibitions include: Kunsthalle Bern, Switzerland 1999; Artsonje Center, Seoul 1998; Projects, Museum of Modern Art, New York, USA 1997; Step by Step, Th-that's..., Il Gallery, Seoul, South Korea 1988.
Group exhibitions include: dAPERTutto, Biennale di Venezia 1999; Hugo Boss Prize, Guggenheim Museum Soho, New York 1998; Fast Forward, The Power Plant Contemporary Art Centre, Toronto, Canada 1997; 4ième Biennale de Lyon, Halle Tony Garnier, Lyon, France 1997; Join Me! Spiral/Wacoal Art Centre, Tokyo, Japan 1996.

Hydra (Monument), 1998
Photoprint on vinyl, inflated by airpumps

LIANG Juhui

Artist born in 1959 in Guanghou, China. Lives and works in Guanghou. Art Director of Guangdong TV since 1982.
Exhibitions include: Another Long March – Chinese Conceptual Art 1997, Breda, The Netherlands, 1997; In the Name of Art, Liuhaishu Museum, Shanghai, 1996; One Hour Game, Guangzhou, 1996; Digital Game, Guanhshou, 1996; Flower on the Human's Skull, Room 14, San Yu Road, Guangzhou, 1995.

One Hour Action/Game; 360 City I
Video, running time 30 minutes; photographs

LIEW Kung Yu

Artist (originally trained as a graphic designer), born in 1960 in Jitra, Malaysia. Lives and works in Kuala Lumpur, Malaysia.

Exhibitions include; The First Asia Pacific Triennial of Contemporary Art, Queensland Art Gallery, Australia, 1993; Temu Seni Multi Media Nur Gora Rupa, Taman Budaya Surakata, Indonesia 1994; Dilating Pupil, Design House Gallery, Berlin, Germany 1995; Art in Southeast Asia 1997: Glimpses into the Future, Museum of Contemporary Art, Tokyo and Hiroshima City Museum of Contemporary Art, Hiroshima, Japan.

Pasti Boleh / Sure You Can, 1997; Selamat Datang to Kuala Lumpur, 1998–99
Installation with red carpet, trophies and photo-booth; collage

Selamat Datang to Malaysia, performance by Lena Ang and Liew Kung Yu in the Louisiana Museum of Modern Art

William LIM

Architect born in 1932 in Hong Kong. William Lim Associates Pte based in Singapore. Trained at the Architectural Association, London and Harvard University. Principal partner of William Lim Associates, Singapore. President of AA Asia, a forum of architectural discourse in Asia; Visiting Professor at the Royal Melbourne Institute of Technology (RMIT), Australia. His writings and lectures deal with the development of architecture and the problems of urbanism in Asia.
Recent publications include: *Contemporary Vernacular: evoking traditions in Asian architecture*, 1997; *Cities for People*, 1990.

City Projects, 1974–99
Plans and photographs

LIN Yilin

Artist born in 1964 in Guangzhou, Guangdong Province, China. Lives and works in Guangzhou.
Exhibitions include: Verpachtetes Erbe-Hong Kong 1997, Museum für Kunsthandwerk, Frankfurt, Germany 1997; Another Long March – Chinese Conceptual Art 1997, Fundament Foundation, Breda, the Netherlands 1997; The First Academic Exhibition of Chinese Contemporary Art, Gallery of the Capital Normal University, Beijing 1996.

The Result of 1000 Pieces, 1999; Safely Manœuvred Through Lin He Street and Driver, 1977–99; X Billion and First Person, 1998
Installation with brick wall; video compilation, running time 30 minutes; photographs

Armin Linke, photograph of Tuk Tuk, Navin Rawanchaikul and Rirkrit Tiravanija

Armin LINKE

Photographer born in 1966. Lives and works in Milan, Italy.
Solo exhibitions include: Ritratti, Galeria Mole, Tokyo 1999; Sozialromantischer Ausblick, Newsantandrea, Savona Galleria Raucci/Santamaria, Naples 1998; Instant Book 1/2/3, J. Deitch, New York 1996; Instant Book 2 (multivision in collaboration with E. Mazzoli, Moderna Galerija Ljubljana, Slovenia 1995; Camera di Sicurezza, Studio Guenzani, Milan 1994.
Group exhibitions include: Imitating Christmas, Wiensowski & Harbord, Berlin 1998; Berlin Biennale 1998; Tratto continuo (multivision from 'Instant Book 1/2/3'), Triennale di Milano 1997; Un secolo di ritratto fotografico in Italia 1895-1995.

Untitled, 1998; Cities on the Move, 1997–99
Photographs; photographs of the installation of Cities on the Move from Vienna, Bordeaux, New York, Copenhagen and London.

LIU Thai Ker

Architect born in 1938 in Singapore. Director of Singapore's RSP Architects Planners and Engineers (Pte) Ltd, and Chairman of the National Arts Council. Formerly the Chief Officer of the Housing and Development Board, and Chief Executive Officer and Chief Planner of the new Urban Redevelopment Authority. Currently planning advisor for 10 cities in China, including Beijing and Tianjin.

City Projects, 1997
Panels and slides

Ken LUM

Artist born in 1959 in Vancouver, Canada. Lives and works in Vancouver.
Solo exhibitions include: Galerie Duchamp, Ecole Municipale d'Arts Plastiques, Yvetot, France 1997; Andrea Rosen Gallery, New York 1997; Stills Gallery, Edinburgh, Scotland 1996.
Group exhibitions include: One Minute Scenario, Le Printemps de Cahors, France 1997; Optimiste, Carreau des Arts-Place de la Fontaine, Cergy-Pontoise, France 1997; Shopping, Deitch Projects, John Delaria, New York 1996.

Souvenirs from all the Chinese restaurants in the world outside China, 1998
Installation with mirrors and postcards – continuous project

Greg LYNN

Architect. Lives and works in Los Angeles, USA. Trained at Miami University (B.Phil. in Philosophy and B.Ed. in Environmental Design, 1986) and Princeton University (March, 1988). Partner with Michael McInturf in FORM, founded 1994. Visiting Assistant Professor at Columbia University, Graduate School of Architecture, Planning and Preservation.
Projects include: Cincinnati Country Day School, Ohio; H2 House for the OMV Corporation, Vienna, Austria; CitronHouse, New York; Port Authority Triple Bridge Gateway Competition.
Publications include: *Animate Form*, 1997; *Lightness*, ANT Magazine no. 5 1993.

The Korean Presbyterian Church of New York, 1997
6 sketch stereolithographs on light box

Fumihiko MAKI

Architect born in 1928 in Tokyo, Japan.
Trained at the University of Tokyo (B.Arch., 1952) and Harvard University Graduate School of Design (M.Arch., 1954). Established Maki and Associates in 1964.
Recent projects include: Tokyo Church of Christ, Tokyo 1995; Fukuoka University Student Centre, Kyushu 1996; Kaze-no-Oka Crematorium, Kyushu 1996; Natori Performing Arts Centre, Miyagi 1997; Nippon Convention Centre 'Makuhari Messe Phase II', Chiba, Japan 1997.

Japanese City Spaces 1969–98; Golgi Structure, 1968
Plans; slides

Fiona MEADOWS/Frédéric NANTOIS

Fiona Meadows, born in 1967, grew up in London and Paris, and studied for 2 years in Japan. Architect DPLG, DEA Architectural and Urban Project, PhD research in the French Institute of Urbanism supervised by Jean-Louis Cohen, Assistant Professor in the School of Architecture of Paris-La Vilette.
Frédéric Nantois, born in 1965, grew up in a Parisian suburb, studied for 2 years in Japan. Architect DPLG, DEA Multimedia Communications and creation, PhD research supervised by Pierre Levy.
Exhibitions include: green and Glocal, Digital city/critical space, Academy of Architecture, Tiburg City Hall, The Netherlands 1997; Incomplete Post-Utopian Tentative 2, Artifice Exhibition, Architecture Foundation, London 1997.

Spaces of non memory places 1997; Per-Ac 1998; Tentative d'épuisement d'un lieu, 1996
Video compilation, running time 36 minutes

Sohn-Joo MINN

Architect born in 1959. Trained at Harvard University Graduate School of Design (M. Arch.). Currently Professor of Architecture at Kyonggi University.
Projects include: Space Design for 2nd Kwangiu Biennale; Chuyang Memorial Training Centre for Missionaries, Sulak; Suh Junggi Fashion Building, Seoul; Chiak Village, Wonju; Sung Rak Won Museum, Seoul; Anderson Graduate School of Management (with I.M. Pei).

Seoul Reading – Seoul Dreaming
Model and drawing

Ryuji MIYAMOTO

Artist born in 1947 in Tokyo. Lives and works in Tokyo.
Solo exhibitions include: Galerie Gilles Peyroulet & Cie, Paris 1998; Centre Nationale de la Photographie, Paris 1998; Octagon, Zeit-Foto Gallery, Tokyo 1998; Cardboard Houses, Yokohama Portside Gallery, Yokohama 1994.
Group exhibitions include: Szenenwechsel XV, Museum für Moderne Kunst, Frankfurt am Main 1999; Et maintenant? Donai Yanen!, Ensba, Paris 1998; Photography and Beyond in Japan, Los Angeles County Museum of Art 1996, Corcoran Gallery of Art, Washington 1996, Denver Art Museum, Honolulu 1997; Sixth International Biennial of Architecture, Venice, Japanese Pavilion (First Prize) 1996.

Kobe 1995 – After the Earthquake, 1995; Cardboard Houses, 1994–96
Photographs

Rudi MOLACEK

Artist born in 1948 in Kindberg, Austra. Lives and works in New York.
Solo exhibitions include: Gasser & Grunert, Cologne 1997; Nanomuseum (touring) with Hans-Ulrich Obrist 1996; Krobath & Wimmer, Vienna 1996.
Group exhibitions include: The Courtyard Gallery, Beijing 1997; Edward Thorpe Gallery, New York 1997; L'Art du Plastique, Ecole Nationale Supérieure des Beaux-Arts, Paris 1996; Sommerlust, Galerie Meile, Luzern 1996.

Cities on the Move, 1997
Billboard poster

Mariko MORI

Artist born in 1967 in Tokyo, Japan. Lives and works in New York.
Solo exhibitions include: Galerie Emmanuel Perrotin, Paris 1996; Centre national d'art contemporain de Grenoble 1996; Made in Japan, Deitch Projects, New York 1996.
Group exhibitions include: Some Kind of Heaven, Kunsthalle Nürnberg 1997; By Night, Fondation Cartier pour l'art contemporain, Paris 1996; The Scream, Arken Museum of Modern Art, Norway 1996; New Histories, The Institute of Contemporary Art, Boston 1996; Ironic Fantasy, The Miyagi Museum of Art.

Takashi MURAKAMI

Artist born in 1962 in Tokyo, Japan. Lives and works in Tokyo and New York.
Solo exhibitions include: Blum and Poe, Santa Monica USA 1997; Emmanuel Perrotin, Paris, France 1997; Konnichiwa, Mr. DOB, Kirin Plaza Osaka 1996.
Group exhibitions incldue: Need for Speed, Grazer Kunstverein, Graz, Austria 1997; Asia-Pacific Triennial, Queensland Art Gallery, Brisbane, Australia 1996; Ironic Fantasy, The Miyagi Museum of Art, Sendal, Miyagi, Japan 1996.

Jumbo; Player; Stew (blue), Wawawa, 1995
Paintings

Matthew NGUI

Artist born in 1962 in Singapore. Lives and works between Singapore and Australia.
Works predominantly with site-specific installations which often include performative or time-based element and address ideas of representation and meaning, cultural derivation and monopoly, opaque and porous boundaries, reality and illusion.
Exhibitions include: Perth Institute of Contemporary Art; Performance Space, Sydney; Singapore Art Museum; 23rd Sao Paulo Biennial; Documenta X, Kassel, Germany 1997.

Installation with with grey pipes, 1999
Site-specific installation linking different parts of the gallery with plumbing pipes

Tsuyoshi OZAWA

Artist born in 1965 in Tokyo. Lives and works in Tokyo.
Has been organising the 'Nasubi Gallery', the world's smallest portable gallery, since 1993, making over 25 exhibitions featuring young artists. Other projects include: Jozoing (1987-) involving over 30 countries; and Sodan-art (1989), a consultative and collaborative project with other artists.

Street Stall Project, 1997
Painted market display stands
Nasubi Galleries, 1999
Individual wall-mounted galleries in milk boxes. Project curated in collaboration with The Institute of International Visual Arts (inIVA). Exhibiting artists: Alistair Raphael, Simon Tegala, Philip Lai, Indika Perera, Susan Pui San Lok, Erika Tan, Cai Yuan, Jian Jun Xi, Mayling To

Ellen PAU

Artist born in 1961 in Hong Kong. Lives and works in Hong Kong.
Work ranges from performing as a Canto-pop singer on MTV to making independent video installations. Founder member of the artists' group Videotage, an active promoter of independent video and film art in Hong Kong. Currently works in a hospital and teaches video at the City University of Hong Kong and the University of Science and Technology.
Exhibitions include: Kwangju Biennale, Korea; Container 96, Copenhagen; Asia-Pacific Triennial, Australia.

Pledge #5, 1997
Video installation

Renzo PIANO

Architect born in 1937 in Genoa. Currently has offices in Genoa, Paris, Berlin and Sydney under the name Renzo Piano Building Workshop.
Completed projects include: Extension, Art Institute of Chicago, USA 1998; Daimler Benz Potsdamer Platz projects, Berlin 1998; Ushibuka Bridge, Kumamoto, Japan 1997; Cy Twombly Pavilion, Houston, USA 1995; Kansai International Airport, Osaka, Japan 1997; Lingotto Concert-Congress Hall, Turin, Italy 1994; Museum for the Menil Collection, Houston, USA 1986; VSS experimental vehicle for FIAT, Turin, Italy 1980.
Projects in progress include: Paul Klee Museum, Bern, Switzerland 1999; urban rehabilitation for the ex-Cantoni area, Legano, Italy 1998; Hermes Tower, Tokyo, Japan 1998; Harvard University Art Museum Master Plan 1997; KPN Telecom Office Tower, Rotterdam, The Netherlands 1997; Interior and exterior rehabilitation of the Pompidou Centre, Paris 1995.

Kansai International Airport – Passenger Terminal Building, 1990
Photographs and plans

TAXI
THE MOVE
ก-9999

Eko PRAWOTO

Architect born in 1958. Lives and works in Yogyakarta, Indonesia.
Trained at the Gadjah Mada University (1982) and the Berlage Institute, Amsterdam (Masters Degree, 1991–1993).
Completed several projects as an architect, including private houses, urban settlements for poor people, campus buildings, offices, churches and an art gallery. In recent years has been working among artists in Yogyakarta, helping them design their houses. Is interested in how to live in the modern world without losing sight of Indonesian tradition and often uses the traditional material of bamboo in new and innovative constructions.

Housing project for the urban poor, Yogyakarta, Indonesia 1993
Drawings, plans, slides

Cedric PRICE

Architect practising in central London since 1960.

Tokyo Forum Competition 1989; City of the Future 1981; Satellite City, Bucks., UK 1980; Magnet – Japanese Panel 1996; Demountable market stall, 1987
Drawings and mixed media panel; market stall

Navin RAWANCHAIKUL and Rirkrit TIRAVANIJA

Navin Rawanchaikul: artist born in 1971 in Chiang Mai, Thailand. Lives and works in Fukuoka, Japan.
Solo exhibitions include: Navin and his Gang (Visit) Vancouver, Contemporary Art Gallery, Vancouver 1997.
Collaborative projects include: Navin Cooperative Society: Sap-Da Ruam-Tuak Tuk Tuk-Koan-Muang (with Rirkrit Tiravanija); 20 Tuk-Tuk Drivers and Muo-Hao-Luk-Kow-Nuang (with Rirkrit Tiravanija, Kosit Juntaratip and Chiang Mai residents), Chiang Mai, Thailand 1997- ; Navin Gallery Bangkok, a series of exhibitions in a taxi (1995-).

Rirkrit Tiravanija: artist born in 1961 in Buenos Aires, Argentina. Lives and works in New York.
Solo exhibitions include: MOMA Project 58, New York 1997; Helga Maria Klosterfeld, Hamburg 1997; Untitled 1996, Loup, est-tu la? Galleria Emi Fontana, Milan, Italy 1996; Untitled 1996 (traffic), Navin Gallery Bangkok 1996.
Group exhibitions include: Letter and Event, Apex Art CP New York 1997; Performance Anxiety, MCA Chicago, IL 1997; Sculpture Projects Münster 1997; A Summer Group Show, Neugerriemschneider, Berlin 1997.

2 Tuk Tuks (Thailand Motorized Three-Wheeler), 1997
Two Thai motorcycle taxis with decorated accessories, cassette players, speakers, advertising panels and postcard boxes; painting and billboard

opposite:
2 Tuk Tuks, 1997, as shown at Louisiana Museum of Modern Art

Jesse REISER & Nanako UMEMOTO

Jesse Reiser, architect born in 1958 in New York, USA; Nanako Umemoto, architect born in Kyoto, Japan.

Tokyo Bay Experiment, 1998
Photographs and text panels

Richard ROGERS

Architect born in 1933 in Florence, Italy. Trained at the Architectural Association in London and at Yale University.
Founded the Richard Rogers Partnersip in 1977. Founding Directors: Richard Rogers, John Young, Marco Goldschmied and Mike Davies.
Major projects include: Law Courts, Bordeaux 1999; the European Court of Human Rights (Strasbourg, 1995); Channel 4 Headquarters, London 1994; Kabucki-Cho Tower, Tokyo 1993; Lloyd's of London, London 1978; Centre Georges Pompidou, Paris (with Renzo Piano) 1971-76.
Urban masterplans include: Pu Dong Financial District, Shanghai; ParcBIT, Majorca; Greenwich Peninsula Site and Millennium Experience, London.

Seoul Broadcasting Centre, Korea 1996–97; Industrialised Housing System, Korea 1992
Models, photographs, drawings

Kazuyo SEIJIMA

Architect born in 1956 in Ibaraki Prefecture, Japan. Lives and works in Tokyo.
Established Kazuyo Seijima & Associates in Tokyo in 1987.
Visiting lecturer at Tokyo Institute of Technology, Japan Women's University and the Science University of Tokyo (1997).
Major works include: Police Box, Chofu Station 1995; World City Expo, Tokyo 1996; A Study for Metropolitan Housing 1995; Pachinko Parlor III 1996.
Projects in collaboration with Ryue Nishizawa include: Multi-Media Studio, 1996; S-House 1996; N-Museum 1997; M-House 1997.

Site plan, 1997; Ushiko office building
Plan; video, running time 8 minutes

SEUNG H-Sang

Architect born in 1952 in Pusan, Korea. Lives and works in Seoul.
Trained at Seoul National University (BA and MA). Worked for Space Group of Korea, founded by the late Kim Swoo Geun, 1974–89. Received the KIA Prize in 1991 and 1992, the Kim Swoo Geun Prize in 1993 and the Grand Prize of Architectural Culture in 1993. Guest lecturer and studio critic at various universities, member of SA (Seoul School of Architecture).
Exhibitions and international forums include: Izmo Architectural Forum; Architects Forum; IAA Exhibition; 4.3 Group Architectural Exhibition.

Beauty of Poverty, Seoul, the City of Memory and Desire, 1997
Plans, sections, elevations and photographs

SHEN Yuan

Artist born in 1959 in Xian You, Fujian, China. Lives and works in Paris.
Exhibitions include: Perdre sa salive, A Vices and Virtues project, Paris, France 1994; Uncertain Pleasure, Art Beatus Gallery, Vancouver 1997; parisien(ne)s, Camden Arts Centre, London 1997; Inclusion/Exclusion, Steirischer Herbst, Graz, Austria 1996; The Fall of Man, Three Rooms & a Kitchen Gallery, Pori, Finland 1995.

Alley-Battle, 1997, as shown at capcMusée d'art contemporain de Bordeaux

Alley-Battle, 1997
Installation with video projection and bicycle-mounted cannons

SHI Yong

Born in 1963 in China. Lives and works in Shanghai, China.
Exhibitions include: Existence and Environment the Chinese Way, the First Academic Exhibition of Chinese Contemporary Art, The Art Museum of Capital Normal University, Beijing 1997; Let's Talk About Money, the First Shanghai International Fax Art Exchanging Exhibition, Shanghai Huashan Art Vocational School Gallery, 1996; In the Name of Art, Chinese Contemporary Art Exchange Exhibition, The Art Museum of Liu Haisu, 1996.
www.shangart.com/shiyong

12 hours Leaping in the City, 1994
Photographic panels

Judy Freya SIBAYAN and Matt GATTON

Judy Freya Sibayan: artist born 1953 in Baguio City, Philippines. Lives and works in Manila.
Solo exhibitions include: Trans Planted Sala/Ob Scene Sofas, Penguin Café Gallery 1985; Dream Objects, Loft Gallery, Otis Art Institute of Parsons School of Design 1983.
Group exhibitions include: Five Women Artists, Pinaglabanan Gallery, Manila 1987; Asian Art Biennial, Dhaka, Bangladesh; Thirteen Artists Retrospective, Culture Centre of the Philippines; Asia City, The Photographers' Gallery, London.
Matt Gatton: artist born in 1967 in Stuttgart, Germany. Lives and works in Manila.
Solo exhibitions include: Breathe, Scapular Gallery Nomad, Manila 1999; Wordsmith, Artswatch, Louisville USA 1997; Heads, Otis B Singletary Center for the Arts, University of Kentucky, USA 1993; Night Visions, University of Louisville, USA.
Group exhibitions include: Philippine Photography Survey, Ayala Museum, Manila, Philippines 1999; Kunst in der Stadt, Frankfurter Hof, Mainz, Germany 1997.

Death of an Airline, 1999
Installation in the form of a bonfire with map, airline flight paths and news cuttings

Drawing for Death of an Airline

Marintan SIRAIT & Andar MANIK

Marintan Sirait: artist born in 1960 in Braunschweig, Germany. Lives and works in Bandung, Indonesia. Andar Manik: artist born in 1959 in Bandung, Indonesia. Lives and works in Bandung.
Selected collaborative exhibitions and performances include: São Paulo Biennial, Brazil 1996; Asia Pacific Triennial, Brisbane, Australia 1996; Indie-Indonesia Festival, The Hague, Netherlands 1995; The International Contemporary Art of the non-alignment countries, Jakarta, Indonesia 1995; Lemah Putih, Solo, Indonesia 1994; Jakarta Biennial of Visual Art, Indonesia 1993-4; Cementi Gallery, Yogyakarta, Indonesia 1993.

Home Body Home, 1997
Installation with hanging bed, map of Indonesia, projection and mud

Home Body Home, 1997, as shown at capcMusée d'art contemporain de Bordeaux

Yutaka SONE

Artist born in 1965. Lives and works in Tokyo, Japan.
Solo exhibitions include: Hiroshima Contemporary Art Museum, Hiroshima 1997; Scoop, Mitaka City Arts Centre, Tokyo 1996; Future Perfect, Tokyu Bunkamara Gallery, Tokyo 1996.
Group exhibitions include: Du Construit, Du Paysage, Centre régional d'art contemporain, Sète, France 1997; Sculpture Projects Münster, Germany 1997; Asian Walking, Shiseido Gallery 1997; Interzones, Kunstforeningen, Copenhagen, Denmark 1996.

Snow Leopard, 1997
marble sculpture
Night Bus, 1997
Video, running time 110 minutes

Snow Leopard, 1997, Collection and courtesy of SHISEIDO ART HOUSE

Margherita SPILUTTINI

Photographer born in 1947 in Schwarzach, Austria. Lives and works in Vienna, Austria. Recent exhibitions include: Transfiction, Galerie Charim Klocker, Vienna; Galerie Fotohof, Salzburg 1997; Photographers of architecture, 6th Biennale for Architecture, Venice 1996. Installation photographer for *Cities on the Move* in Vienna.

Cities on the Move at Vienna Secession, 1997
Slides

Manit SRIWANICHPOOM

Artist born in 1961. Lives and works in Bangkok.
Group exhibitions include: the First Fukuoka Art Triennale, Fukuoka, Japan 1999; XXIV Biennial International de Sao Paolo, Brazil 1998; Contemporary Color Photography from Asia, the Photographic Resource Center, Boston USA 1998; Asia City, The Photographers' Gallery, London 1998; Photographies des 3 Continents, Nantes, France 1997; Asiatica, Phnom Penh, Cambodia 1997; One day of my life in a box, Bangkok and Germany 1996-97.
Film and video art includes: *Pink Man on Tour*, VDO art 1998; *Uk-ka-bat (meteorite)*, 16mm experimental film 1995; *Land of Laugh*, 16mm experimental film 1992.

This Bloodless War, 1997
Photographs

SUPERFLEX

Group of artists based living and working in Denmark.
Solo exhibitions include: karlsrona2/Utrecht, Casco Gallery, Utrecht, Holland 1999; Superflex Biogas in Africa (new life), Hillside Gallery, Tokyo, Japan 1999, Artspace, Sydney Australia 1999, Acsess local, Paris 1998, Museum of Contemporary Art Helsinki 1997; Orange Sauna, Service Gallery, Stockholm 1996.
Recent group exhibitions include: 3 public projects, Karlsrona, Sweden 1999; Something rotten, Museum Friedericianum, Kassel 1998; Bicycle Thieves, Monk Parakeet (Dan Peterman), Chicago 1998; Never Been in a Riot, Transmission Gallery, Glasgow 1998.
Music: Music System 1, Workshop in Stockholm organised within Art genda, Stockholm 1998; Music System 2, installation at Roskilde Frestival 1998; Music System 3, Installation at 'Freilufts musik', organised by Ursula Block, Gelbe Musik, Mon 1998; Starting a music label with August Engkilde: Superflex Music, Copenhagen 1997; Hello DJ, cd, Superflex Music, Copenhagen 1997; The Tag, Music video production, California 1997

www.superflex.dk

Aaron TAN

Architect born in 1963 in Singapore. Director of OMA Asia, founded with Rem Koolhaas in 1994.
Publications/lectures/exhibitions include: Kwangju Biennale, South Korea 1997; AA Asia, Beijing 1997; SD 01/97, Japan 1997; On-site critic, Harvard/Hong Kong 1996; Kikukawa Vol 4, Japan 1996; Kowloon Walled City, (book) 1997.
Projects in progress include: in Hong Kong – Electric Road Office Building I&II, Queen's Road East Office; in Singapore – Elizabeth Residential Tower; in China – Shenzhen Theme World mixed use Master Plan.

City on Fire, 1998
Slide and audio installation

Fiona TAN

Artist born in 1966 in Indonesia. Grew up in Australia. Lives and works in the Netherlands.
Solo exhibitions include: Galerie O Zwei, Berlin, Germany 1996; Die Weibe Galerie Cologne, Germany 1995; Artspace Witzerhausen, Amsterdam, The Netherlands 1995.
Group exhibitions include: De Appel, Hong Kong Perfumed Harbour, Stedelijk Museum, Amsterdam, The Netherlands 1997; The Secanade, Paris, France; Art(s) d'Europe?, Stedelijk Museum Bureau, Amsterdam, and Fondation Royaumont, Asnières-sur-Oise, France 1997; Hong Kong etc, Johannesburg Biennale 1997.

May You Live in Interesting Times, 1997
Video, running time 60 minutes

Still from May You Live in Interesting Times, 1997.

Takahiro TANAKA

Artist born in 1962 in Shiga, Japan. Lives and works in Tokyo, Japan.
Solo exhibitions include: Tanishima Gallery, Tokyo 1993; Aki-eX Gallery, Tokyo 1993; Curator's Eye 95, Gallery NW House, Tokyo 1995; Criterium 95, Contemporary Art Centre, Art Tower Mito, 1995; Gallery alphaM, Tokyo 1996.

Fragments of eyes, 1985–97
Slide projection

TAY Kheng Soon

One of the most influential Singaporean architects. He and his firm Architecture Tanaga have played an important role in the Asian architectural and cultural scene. As an architectural theorist, he has also widely published his critique of Western Modernism. With profound understanding of the Asian context, he intensively promotes alternative ideas to the established mode of urban development in Asia. His work and ideas have been very influential in the current debates on urban growth in Asia.

Kampong Bugis Development Guide Plan
Photographs

Chandraguptha THENUWARA

Artist born in 1960 in Galle, Sri Lanka. Lives and works in Sri Lanka.
Director of the Vbhavi Academy of Fine Arts and visiting lecturer at the Institute of Aesthetic Studies.
Solo exhibitions include: Barrelism & Other Works, the Heritage Gallery, Columbo 1997; In Spacetime, the British Council, Kandy, and the National Art Gallery, Columbo 1995.
Group exhibitions include: Artists Camp Exhibition, National Art Gallery, Columbo 1997; Vibhavi Academy of Fine Arts First Annual, National Art Gallery, Columbo 1997; Women in Art, Mountcastle Gallery 1996.

Barrelism Tourist Map, 1997
Drawings and barrel

Barrelism Tourist Map, 1997

TSANG Tsou-choi

Street calligrapher born in 1921 in Liantang Village, Guangdong Province.
Has worked as a farmer, a steward in a weaving factory, a labourer transporting water pipes and as a caretaker in a rubbish collection station. He married in 1956, and has since been writing grafitti on street walls, claiming to be the 'King of Kowloon'. According to him, he has read through the ancestral book of his family and discovered that much of the land in Kowloon belonged to his ancestors, but was annexed for the use of the Hong Kong government with no compensation offered. This prompted him to write graffiti expressing his discontent.

Street calligraphy of Tsang Tsou-choi
Photographs

USHIDA FINDLAY

Architecture practice based in Tokyo and London.
Eisaku Ushida: born in Japan, trained at the University of Tokyo. Has worked with Arata Isozaki and Associates, Richard Rogers (The Lloyd's Building) and Alan Stanton.
Kathryn Findlay: born in Scotland, trained at the Architectural Association, London. Worked for Arata Isozaki and Associates before setting up her own practice. Currently Associate Professor of Architecture at Tokyo University (the first foreign woman ever to hold such a post).
Competitions and awards include: Homes for the Future, Glasgow City of Architecture 1998, commissioned winner; Financial Times Millennium Bridge Competition, shortlisted; Annual Architectural Design Commendation of the Architectural Institute of Japan 1996.
Recent exhibitions include: Concept House, The Architecture Foundation, London 1998; 1009 Footpath, Adelaide Festival installation, Australia 1996; Parallel Landscapes, Gallery MA, Tokyo 1996.

Photo: © Katsuhisa Kida

Truss Wall House, 1991–93
Model and photographs

WANG Du

Artist born in 1956 in Hubei, China. Lives and works in Paris.
Solo exhibitions include: Les Travaux du corps, Gate Foundation, Amsterdam 1997; Reliques, a Vices & Virtues Project, Paris 1994.
Group exhibitions include: Uncertain Pleasure, Art Beatus Gallery, Vancouver 1997; Soap, Anthropological Museum, Rotterdam 1997; Kulturschmiede, Frankfurt 1996.

International Landscape, 1997; Alarm Tower, 1998–99
Plaster figure of prostitute; watch tower with street sounds

WANG Jian Wei

Artist born in 1958 in Sichuan Province, China. Lives and works in Beijing Province, China.
Exhibitions include: Documenta X, Kassel, Germany 1997; Another Long March – Chinese Conceptual Art 1997, Breda, The Netherlands 1997; Journey to the East, Art Centre of Hong Kong University of Science and Technology, Hong Kong 1997; The 2nd Asia-Pacific Triennial of Contemporary Art, Queensland Art Gallery, Australia 1996; Kwangju Biennial – infloART Kwangju, Korea 1995.

Missing, 1997
Installation with name cards, photographs and text

WANG Jia Qiang

Architect living and working in Zhuhai, China.

Zhuhai Airport
Photographs and plans

opposite:
Wang Du, Alarm Tower, 1998-99, as shown at Louisiana Museum of Modern Art

Neon Urlaub, 1997

Jun-Jieh WANG

Artist born in 1963 in Taipei. Lives and works between Taiwan and Berlin.
Solo exhibitions include: Neon Urlaub – Agency Version, Agfa Gallery, Goethe Institute, Hong Kong 1997; neon – Expo Version, Information Science and Technology Exhibitions Centre, Taipei 1997; Little Mutton Dumplings for the Thirteenth Day, Taipei Fine Arts Museum.
Group exhibitions include: Venice Biennale 1997; Asia Edge '96, Tokyo 1996; Taipei Biennial: The Quest for Identity, Taipei Fine Arts Museum 1996.

Neon Urlaub, 1997
Multi-media projection, running time 120 minutes
www.icfde/neonurlaub

Vitrine of Contemporary Events, 1998 (detail)

WONG Hoy Cheong

Artist born in Penang, Malaysia. Studied fine art, literature and education in the USA. His work in the 1990s has been inter-disciplinary, involving areas such as drawing, installation, performance, video and theatre. His recent works, Lalang (a weed in Malaysia) and of Migrants and Rubber Trees, have explored the linkages in the history and migration of people and plants, the issues of origins, authenticity and assimilation/hybridity.

Seeds of Change, 1997; Vitrine of Contemporary Events, 1998
Installation with café tables, maps of Indonesia, food (on show in Habitat, Tottenham Court Road, London); participatory political sculpture in vitrine

WONG Kar-Wai

Still from Chungking Express, 1992

Film maker born in 1958 in Shanghai, China.
One of a new generation of Hong Kong film makers.
Works include: *As Tears Go By*, 1988; *Days of Being Wild*, 1990 (winner of 5 Hong Kong Film Awards, including Best Film. Best Direction and Best Actor, for Leslie Cheung); *Ashes of Time*, 1992 (winner of Best Cinematography at the 1994 Venice Film Festival); *Chungking Express*, 1992 (Wong's biggest international hit to date); *Fallen Angels*, 1995; *Happy Together*, 1997 (winner of Best Director Award at the Cannes Film Festival).

Chungking Express, 1992
Film, running time 100 minutes

WONG & OUYANG

One of the biggest architectural firms in Hong Kong. Founded in 1972, they have realised major architectural works in Hong Kong, China and other countries in the Pacific Region.
Works include: One Pacific Place; Lippo Centre; Whampoa Garden; Hong Kong's New Convention Centre.

City projects
Photographs, text

XU Tan

Artist born in 1957 in Wuhan, Hubei Province, China. Lives and works in Guangzhou.
Exhibitions include: Another Long March – Chinese Conceptual Art 1997, Breda, The Netherlands 1997; problem 1, Heinrich Böll Stiftung, International Artists' Residency Program, Gothaer Kunstforum, Cologne, Germany 1997; Container 96 – Art Across Oceans, Langelinic, Copenhagen, Denmark 1996; Possibility, Zhong Guang Building, Guangzhou 1996.

Made in China – Beijing, Shanghai, Guangzhou, Shenzhen, 1998
Slide and video installation with plaster fruits

Riken YAMAMOTO

Architect born in 1945 in Beijing, China. Trained at Nihon University and Tokyo National University of Fine Art and Music. Established Riken Yamamoto & Field Shop in 1973. Has received numerous awards including: 1st prize in the competition for Iwadeyama Junior High School, the competition for Saitama Prefectural University of Nursing and Welfare, the competition for Hiroshima Nishi Fire Station and the competition for Hakodate Municipal College, none of which have yet been realised.

Untitled, 1999
Slide installation

Miwa YANAGI

Detail from Elevator Girl House 1F, 1997

Artist born in Kobe City, Japan. Lives and works in Tokyo.
Solo exhibitions include: Gallery Muramatsu, Tokyo 1997; Looking for the Next Story, Gallery Sowaka, Kyoto 1994.
Group exhibitions include: Moment Ginza, Forgfabriken, Stockholm 1997; du construit, du paysage, Centre régional d'art contemporain, Sète, France 1997; Future Recollections, Kyoto Art Museum 1997; Lust und Leere, Japanische Photographie der Gegenwart, Kunsthalle Wien 1997.

Info – town – garden fountain – brilliant woods – elevator, 1996; The house of the woman of the elevator 1F, 1997
Photographs

Ken YEANG

Architect born in 1948 in Penang, Malaysia. Lives and works in London. Corporate Member of the Royal Institute of British Architects, a member of other institutes as well as Professor at Sheffield University, UK. His special area of interest is in the design of ecologically-responsive buildings, such as skyscrapers. He has designed and built a number of 'bioclimatic skyscrapers'. In 1995 his firm, TR Hamzah and Yeang, received the Aga Khan Award for Architecture for their Menara Mesiniaga skyscraper.

Bioclimatic Skyscraper, 1999
Model

YIN Xiuzhen

Artist born in 1963 in Beijing, China. Lives and works in Beijing.
Solo exhibitions include: Ruined Capital, Gallery of Capital University, Beijing 1996; Yin Xiuzhen's Art, Contemporary Art Gallery, Beijing 1995.
Group exhibitions include: Another Long March – Chinese Conceptual Art 1997, Fundament Foundation, Chasse Kazerne, Breda, The Netherlands 1997; Immutability and Fashion – Chinese Contemporary Art in the Midst of Changing Surroundings, Kirin Art Space Harajuku, Tokyo; Kirin Plaza, Osaka; Altium, Fukuoka, Japan 1997.

Doors, 1998
Installation of 46 black & white photographs on hinged wooden panels

Yin Xiuzhen,
Ruined Capital, 1996

YUAN Shun

Artist born in 1961 in Shanghai. Lives and works in Berlin.
Solo exhibitions include: Summer Cinema, Atelierhaus Worpswede Za Moca Foundation Tokyo, Japan 1999; Hin und Her, Museum of Art, Shanghai, Hong Kong Arts Centre, Goethe Institute Hong Kong 1998; Haupt Stadt I DAAD, Asian Fine Arts Factory, Berlin 1998; The Trinity, Künstlerhaus Bethanien, Berlin 1994.
Group exhibitions include: Asian Art Now, Fine Art Factory, Berlin 1998; Station Deutschland, Künstlerhaus Bethanien, Berlin 1995–96; Construction in Process IV, My home is your home, Lodz, Poland 1993; China Avant-Garde, National Art Museum Beijing 1989.

Haupt Stad i, 1997
Postcard
Beyond the Boundary, 1999
Video, running time 10 minutes

ZHAN Wang

Artist born in 1962 in Beijing, China. Lives and works in Beijing.
Exhibitions include: Chinese Contemporary Art Exhibition, Tokyo Watari-um Gallery of Contemprary Art 1997; Forever Return – 97 South Mountain Sculpture Studio 1997; 1996; International Sculpture Wild-open Show, Uminonakamichi Seaside Park, Fukuoka, Japan 1996; The First Academic Exhibition of Chinese Contemporary Art, Hing Kong Art Centre 1996.

New Map of Beijing: Capital of Today and Tomorrow – Rebuilding the Rockery, 1997; Cleaning the Ruins, 1997
Photographs, maps and texts; photographs

ZHANG Peili

Artist born in 1957 in Hangzhou, China. Lives and works in Hangzhou.
Solo exhibitions include: Galerie Krinzinger, Vienna, Austria 1997; The Art Gallery of Chualongkorn University, Bangkok, Thailand 1997.
Group exhibitions include: Uncertain Pleasure, Art Beatus Gallery, Vancouver 1997; Biennale de Lyon, Maison de Lyon, France 1997; Another Long March – Chinese Conceptual Art 1997, Fundament Foundation, Chasse Kazerne, Breda, The Netherlands 1997; Art 27'96 (Video Forum) Messe Basel, Basel, Switzerland 1996.

Focal Distance, 1996
8 channel video installation with 8 monitors

ZHENG Guogu

Artist born in 1970 in Yangjiang/Guangdong, China. Lives and works in Yangjiang.
Exhibitions include: Contemporary Photographic Art from the PR China, Neuer Berliner Kunstverein 1997; Possibility, Guangzhou 1996; Honeymoon, installation with Big Tail Elephant Group 1996; No Room, China International Art Expo, Guangzhou 1994; Priority Construction, installation with Big Tail Elephant Group 1994; Hammo New Art Special Show, Guangzhou 1994; New Artwork Concepts, Hanmo Art Centre, Beijing 1994.

Impermissible Behaviour of Youth in Yangjiang, 1996
Photographs

ZHOU Tiehai

Artist born in 1966 in Shanghai, China. Lives and works in Shanghai.
Solo exhibitions include: Too Materialistic, Too Spiritualised, Cifa Gallery, Beijing 1996.
Group exhibitions include: Another Long March – Chinese Conceptual Art 1997, Fundament Foundation, Chasse Kazerne, Breda, The Netherlands 1997; promenade in Asia, Shiseido Gallery, Tokyo, Japan 1997; In the Name of Art, Liu Haisu Art Museum, Shanghai 1996.

Will, 1997
Video, running time 19 minutes

ZHU Jia

Artist born in 1963 in Beijing, China. Lives and works in Beijing.
Group exhibitions include: Uncertain Pleasure, Art Beatus Gallery, Vancouver 1997; Another Long March – Chinese Conceptual Art 1997, Fundament Foundation, Chasse Kazerne, Breda, The Netherlands 1997; Image and Phenomena, The Gallery of China Academy of Fine Arts, Hangzhou, China 1996; Hanmo Gallery, Beijing China 1993.

Forever, 1994
Video projection shot on tricycle-mounted camera, running time 30 minutes

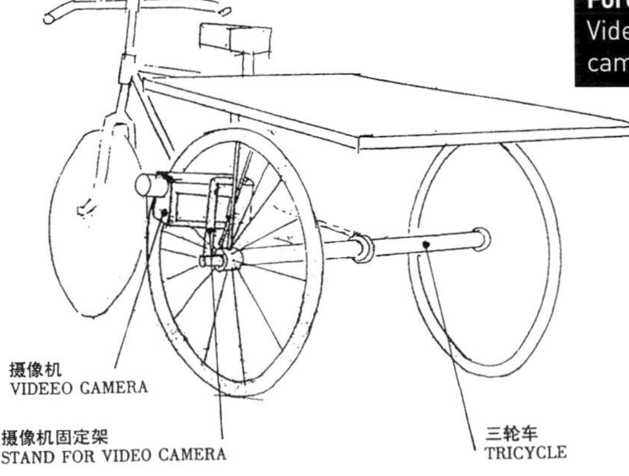

Zhu Jia, working drawing for Forever, 1994

VIDEO
Burberry
指定歐洲英國華人代理商
YEAR OF THE RABBIT
T-SHIRTS SOLD HERE
LONDON
0171-437-6266
OLDEN GATE
GROCERS
金門行
EAT AS MUCH AS YOU LIKE
MONGOLIAN
BUFFET

London on the Move

THE IMPACT OF EAST ASIAN CULTURE IN AND AROUND THE CITY

Julia Diamantis

London is a city on the move; it's evolving. As people from all over the world settle in the city, it grows and moves on. Each immigrant population brings its own food, shops, customs, religions and art forms which enrich the cultural diversity of the existing city. It is this evolution that makes London so rich, vibrant and inspiring, despite its problems. There is a special pride in coming from London which in some respects supersedes ideas of nationhood. There are few places in the world with such an exciting ethnic mix.

This section celebrates East Asian culture in London. It looks at the impact immigration from East Asia has had on the city's cultural landscape. Obviously there has been a history of racial tension but, whilst we do not wish to dismiss the very real problems which continue to exist, 'London on the Move' focuses on the positive cultural effects of the ethnographic mix.

photographs: Julian Anderson

Over the past twenty years the choice of East Asian food in the capital has exploded

Some communities, like the Chinese, have been in London for over 200 years and have exerted a huge influence on the capital – the Chinese takeaway, for example, is as much part of British life as the chip shop once was. Other more recently arrived communities are less widespread and their traditions have yet to enter the mainstream but their presence adds to the cultural wealth of the city.

The nationalities which make up East Asia, from Japan to the Philippines, from China to Indonesia, are culturally very diverse. The area is vast and spreads right around the Pacific Basin. There are about 70,000 people of Chinese origin in London but only around 750 from Taiwan, 25,000 from Japan and about 10,000 from Thailand, not to mention Vietnamese, Indonesians, Filipinos and so on. To complicate matters, there are about 60 million Chinese expatriates living outside China in the other South East Asian countries. This migration has blurred the cultural boundaries. Bring all this to London and the result is a rich mixture of ideas, customs and people with Eastern and Western cultures mingling and fusing,

forming something totally new; the city's cultural identity really is on the move.

People have been settling in London from abroad for centuries, dating back to the Romans. The first major community in London from East Asia were Chinese sailors, recruited by the East India Company, who made their home in the docklands area. By the end of the 19th century, there was a small community of Chinese in Limehouse, although evidence of the Chinatown there remains only in some street names in the area: Ming Street, Canton Street, Peking Street.

The East End and the docklands were the first home for many ethnic groups in the city. As the docks closed, more recent communities have sprung up near Heathrow Airport. New immigrants frequently stay with friends or relatives already living here and communities soon develop; shops, temples, mosques and social clubs open. Take, for example, the Korean community in New Malden with its Buddhist temple, Catholic church and many Korean-owned businesses. These communities often disperse as second and third generation immigrants embrace and become absorbed by the rest of London. In doing so, these individuals bring elements of their heritage into the mainstream. The effect of this cultural infusion means, for example, that pubs serve Tiger Beer alongside pints of bitter, GPs recommend acupuncture to those who wish to stop smoking, and Japanese chic is highly fashionable in many areas of popular culture.

It would be impossible to encompass the complexities of East Asian cultural influence in London in a book of this size. Any attempt to produce a definitive guide would inevitably be incomplete. East Asian cultures are not preserved here, and London is not a static place; East and West interact and produce something new. What follows is only a taste of the wealth of activity which exists. It is a subjective sample. This part of the book reflects the journey we took during our research. And that journey, of course, continues as the city itself moves on.

CHINATOWN, LONDON

photograph: Julian Anderson

WARDOUR STREET

GERRARD STREET

Left side:
- Gerrard's Corner Restaurant
- Hong Kong Bank Offices
- London Chinatown Restaurant
- Golden Dragon Restaurant
- Anglo-Chinese Consultancy
- Royal Dragon Restaurant
- Loon Tao Restaurant
- CD News Music & newsagents
- New Hong Kong Printers
- New Hoo Wah Restaurant
- Phoenix Restaurant
- Luxuriance Restaurant
- New Fook Lam Moon Restaurant
- Lido Restaurant
- New Loon Fung Restaurant
- Loon Fung Supermarket
- Chinese Community Centre
- Hong Kong Cultural Centre
- Harbour City Restaurant
- Friendly Inn Restaurant
- King's Head Public House

Right side:
- Amusement Arcade
- Kowloon Restaurant
- Taoist and Buddhist International Association
- Yee Tung Restaurant
- Le Salon Hair Studio
- Capital Properties
- Yeung's Financial Management
- Tai Kai Lok Restaurant
- Hong Kong Bank
- Lee Ho Fook Restaurant
- Chinese Gift Shop
- Ever Travel Travel Agents
- Cheung Ling Solicitors
- Dumpling Inn Restaurant / Evertours Ltd Travel Services

MACCLESFIELD STREET

- Ying Hwa Bookstore / Nielsen Consultants
- Far East Restaurant
- Dragon Inn Restaurant
- Aroma Restaurant
- Hands Design
- Gerrard's Press
- Top Ten Hair Salon
- New Loon Moon Supermarket
- Mandarin Restaurant
- Shanghai Beauty Salon
- Jen Restaurant
- J F Trading Gifts
- Sound of China Music
- Lok Ho Fook Restaurant
- Shanghai Great China Hairdressers
- Fong, Baldwin and Co Solicitors
- China China Restaurant

source: Chinatown OnLine

Eating →

East Asian food has had a far-reaching influence on London, but is it 'authentic' any more?

East Asian cooking has been accepted by the British more readily than any other aspect of the culture. Not only is the Chinese takeaway a familiar feature of every high street in the country, but Oriental cuisine has had considerable impact on home cooking, not to mention the popularity of the pot noodle and the lunchtime supermarket sushi pack. London supports an enormously diverse collection of East Asian restaurants, as well as many others which draw on Oriental influences.

Paradoxically, it could be argued that the most powerful influence from East Asia on life in Britain is what some consider to be emblematic of British culture: tea. The British even went to war over it. By the late 18th century tea, imported from the East, had become a national obsession. To balance the consequent trade deficit with China, Britain promoted the export of opium from British-ruled India to China. When the Chinese Government tried to put a stop to it, the British declared war – the Opium Wars of 1842-60. Hong Kong became a British colony as a result of these wars and when communist China was closed to the world in the 1950s, Hong Kong Chinese were free to come to Britain, greatly swelling the existing Chinese community in London.

The assimilation of Chinese food into London culture first started during the Second World War. Although there had been restaurants catering for the small Chinese population in the East End since the late 19th century, Chinese restaurants first started to open in Soho in the early 1940s in response to demand from British soldiers who had experienced Chinese food overseas and American soldiers who were already familiar with it back home. However, it was the subsequent changing attitudes to diet and eating out in the 1970s which really established Chinatown and its restaurants. This in turn created the demand for the range of international restaurants which exist now throughout London: Japanese, Vietnamese, Thai, Malaysian and more.

While many East Asian restaurants have adapted their menus to accommodate Western tastes, interestingly this is changing as Londoners become more experienced with East Asian food and seek out the 'authentic'. The popularity of restaurant chains such as Wok Wok and Wagamama and the dramatic rise in the availability of Thai food demonstrate the continuing acceptance of East Asian cuisine.

Just as a glance down any of London's high streets reveals an astonishing range of Asian restaurants, so too a look at the contents of shopping baskets displays an equally interesting selection of Oriental cooking ingredients and pre-cooked meals.

Food is probably the most visible consequence of the cultural exchange between East Asia and Britain. And although some of the rarer dishes and ingredients may still be unknown to the majority of Londoners, this too is changing with attitudes and availability.

FOOD STORES

Sri Thai Oriental Food Centre
56 Shepherds Bush Road, W6
0171 602 0621
A local Thai supermarket which serves the Thai community in West London, specialising in Thai ingredients and products. This is also a good place to find imported Thai magazines and newspapers

Wang Thai
101 Kew Road, SW15
0181 332 2959
Wang Thai imports fresh vegetables and fruit from Thailand every week. It also stocks a wide range of groceries not just from Thailand but also from China, Japan, Vietnam and all over East Asia, along with cooking equipment and imported Thai newspapers and magazines

Hopewell Emporium
2F Dyne Road, NW6
0171 624 5473
Fresh vegetables and groceries mainly from Indonesia but also from the rest of the South East Asia region

Sunrise Oriental Supermarket
41 Vivian Avenue, NW4
0181 202 0321
Food store specializing in Malay and Indonesian cooking ingredients including fresh spices from Malaysia. Across the road, under the same ownership, is the

Oriental Hawkers Delight, a South East Asian fast food takeaway/café where the food is cooked in the front of the shop. Many of the dishes are highly spiced and in no way adapted to Western tastes

Oriental City Plaza
399 Edgware Road, NW9
0181 200 0009
Major oriental shopping centre which has a food court and supermarket selling a wide choice of oriental cooking ingredients

Miura Japanese Food
44 Coombe Road, Kingston
0181 549 8076
Specializes in Japanese groceries but also serves takeaway sushi on Saturday and Sunday lunchtimes, attracting a mixed crowd

Arigato
48-50 Brewer Street, W1
0171 287 1722
Japanese supermarket which also stocks Korean goods and hardly any Western food. There's a lunchtime sushi bar and Arigato also sells Japanese newspapers and magazines from both the UK and Japan

Wing Yip
544 Purley Way, Croydon
0181 688 4880
The largest oriental supermarket in London, stocking groceries and cooking equipment from all over East Asia

Intel Supermarket
126 Malden Road, New Malden
0181 942 9552
Japanese and Korean groceries, vegetables and meats with sushi to take away

RESTAURANTS

Chinese & Taiwanese

Four Seasons
84 Queensway, W2
0171 229 4320
Especially recommended for its boneless duck

Hunan
51 Pimlico Road, SW1
0171 730 5712
Traditional Taiwanese/Chinese food, but there are dishes on the Chinese-language menu that don't appear on the English one, so get the waiter to explain what's on offer or go for the special of the day

Mandarin Kitchen
14 Queensway, W2
0171 727 9012
Great for seafood, the lobster noodles in particular

Man Fu Kung
29 Leicester Square, WC2
0171 727 9012
One of the best – and largest – Chinatown restaurants

Dim sum restaurants

China City
25a Lisle Street, WC2
0171 734 3388
Set back from the road in its own little courtyard, China City seats 500 and is one of the more upmarket restaurants in Chinatown. For those who want a little privacy, there are also four private function rooms where diners can make use of the Karaoke machines

Kam Tong
59 Queensway, W2
0171 229 6065
Dim sum served every day between 12:00 and 17:00

photographs: Julian Anderson

TOURING PARTY WELCOME
歡迎外賣
TAKE AWAY IS WELCOME

Royal China
13 Queensway, W2
0171 221 2535
One of the more expensive Chinese restaurants in Queensway but definitely worth the treat

Thai

Esarn Kheaw
314 Uxbridge Road, W12
0181 743 8930
North Eastern Thai food which is much spicier than the usual Thai food served in London. Esarn Kheaw is highly rated by the city's Thai population

Filipino

Josephine's Restaurant
4 Charlotte Street, W1
0171 580 6551
Josephine's was the first Filipino restaurant in London and is still one of only a handful. Although some of the dishes sound Chinese, they're actually quite different

Indonesian

New Jakarta
150 Shaftesbury Avenue, WC2
0171 836 2644
The New Jakata has been open for many years and although it's bright it has a relaxing mood. One of the owners comes from Sumatra and the cooking has a very authentic feel. For those new to Indonesian cooking there is a set meal made up of a number of small dishes which allows you to sample a wider selection than going for a starter and main course. If you would rather opt for a large main course, try the fish and seafood, both of which are especially good

Melati
21 Great Windmill Street, W1
0171 437 2745
A little dusty looking from the outside but nicer inside and often busy, Melati serves great low-budget Indonesian food

Nusa Dua
11 Dean Street, W1
0171 437 3559
Although bang in the middle of trendy Soho, Nusa Dua feels more like a local restaurant, with incredibly friendly staff. The decor is a little twee, but it is a good place to go for Javanese food

Myanmar (Burma)

Mandalay
444 Edgware Road, W2
0171 258 3696
There cannot be many locations as unprepossessing as 444 Edgware Road. Five minutes north of Edgware Road tube, Mandalay looks like a café rather than a restaurant and stands in stark contrast to the slick chrome and primary colours of the New Cultural Revolution noodle and dumpling bar next door. But it is one of the few places in London which specializes in Burmese food

Singaporean

Bugis Street Cafe
Gloucester Hotel
4-18 Harrington Gardens, SW7
0171 411 4234
Bugis Street is one of Singapore's few remaining 'hawker centres' where stall holders vie with each other for customers who sit at centrally-located municipal tables, eating from paper plates with disposable chop sticks. The Bugis Street Café, being part of the hotel, is altogether a more restrained environment but still serves good Singaporean food

Singapore Garden Two
154 Gloucester Place, NW1
0171 723 8233
Well-established restaurant serving excellent Singaporean food

Malaysian

Mawar
175a Edgware Road, W2
0171 262 1663
Both the buffet and restaurant serve excellent authentic Malaysian cooking

Satay Bar
447-450 Coldharbour Lane, SW9
0171 326 5001
Very stylish, very modern

Satay House
13 Sale Place, W2
0171 723 6763
Satay is the speciality, but try some of the other fantastic Malaysian dishes too. The 'fermented durians cooked with petai, anchovies and turmeric leaves' may be best avoided by those not familiar with the pungent durian fruit. Malaysians are fanatical about the durian, calling it the 'king of fruits'

Makan
270 Portobello Road, W10
0181 960 5169
Makan, which means 'eat' in Malay, is really a lunchtime café but it is soon to open in the evenings as well

photographs: Julian Anderson

Japanese

Mitsukoshi Restaurant
14 Regent Street, W1
0171 930 0317
Japanese restaurant within a department store which generally caters for Japanese tourists

Wagamama
10a Lexington Street, W1
0171 292 0990
4 Streatham Street, WC1
0171 323 9223
101 Wigmore Street, W1
0171 409 0111
Japanese noodles in a contemporary setting. All branches share a minimalist, canteen-like aesthetic but they can be noisy and no bookings mean that queues can be long. They're certainly not intimate but the portions are generous and the prices reasonable. Japanese style bought wholesale by hip young Londoners

Yo! Sushi
52 Poland Street, W1
0171 287 0443
Not just a restaurant but a lifestyle brand – they sell t-shirts, baby-grows and will deliver on specially-imported Japanese bikes. With possibly the world's longest sushi conveyor belt (60m) and robotic drinks trolleys with attitude

Vietnamese

Nam Bistro
326 Upper Street, N1
0171 354 0851

Hai-Ha
206 Mare Street, E8
0181 985 538
Excellent Vietnamese food in a café environment

Korean

Busan
43 Holloway Road, N7
0171 607 8264
Busan, frequented by Gilbert & George, looks a mess from the outside and seems to have missed out on Islington gentrification but it's easy-going, and unpretentious

Jin
16 Bateman Street, W1
0171 734 0908
A place to eat in the evening, Jin is painted matt black and is very dark. Each table has a hidden burner in the middle where food is cooked in front of you

You Me House
96 Burlington Road, New Malden, Surrey
0181 715 1079
Popular with the Korean community in New Malden, You Me House specializes in home cooking

Japanese style is bought wholesale by hip Londoners – but heavily influenced by European values too

Trading

A two-way infusion of cultures, traditions and attitudes

Trading is a two-way process with mutual benefit. As those from East Asia who have settled in London have adopted the fashions, styles, eating and shopping habits of the UK, there has been a corresponding transmission of some Asian customs and values to indigenous Londoners. A dynamic trade of ideas and influences has developed.

Most East Asians living in London actively participate in and contribute to the existing Western culture of the city. Shopping in M&S, visiting the local cineplex, and watching BBC1 are simply aspects of everyday living in the UK. However, it would be overly simplistic not to recognize that for immigrant communities there is also a strong desire to honour and maintain the values and traditions of their parents' communities. As a consequence, there are many examples of organisations, shops and services in London which provide a focus for traditional Asian culture.

The Japan Society, for example, promotes and supports Japanese culture for Japanese people in London. The Singapore UK Association has a newsletter and organises social events for anyone with a connection to Singapore. The Korean community, being fairly autonomous, has a residents' society, a cultural institute and a business association. There are over 50 Chinese community groups and associations in London, ranging from the British Association Of Writers In The Chinese Language to associations of clansmen which organise social events for groups with the same family heritage or surname, such as the Cheung's Clansmen Welfare (Europe) Association.

For newer immigrant communities, the ethnic supermarket often represents much more than simply a place to buy food. It can be a meeting place, sometimes a café, with imported newspapers and magazines for sale, and films on video for hire. The more established communities from East Asia – the Japanese and Chinese communities – have a much stronger presence in London and this is reflected in the more specialist shops which exist. There are, for example, a number of bookshops specializing in Japanese-language publications and Charing Cross Library has a significant collection of Chinese-language books for loan.

Language is an important factor in the maintenance of cultural heritage and ethnic language classes are often organised by community centres. First generation Chinese in London often fear the loss of the mother-tongue in younger generations; traditionally it is seen as the vehicle by which to transmit the ancestral culture from one generation to the next. Nearly half the Chinese in London are British-born and there are over 80 Chinese language classes and supplementary schools in London. The Chinese Chamber Of Commerce in Soho is the largest Chinese language school in Europe.

On the other hand, there is much East Asian culture which has been so absorbed into the British mainstream that it is sometimes difficult to recognize its origins – from Japanese-style shoes to kites. East Asian food shops are patronized by Londoners of all nationalities. Traditional Chinese medicinal treatments are widely employed. There are over 800 registered acupuncturists in London.

Martial Arts have been studied and practised here for decades, with 33 clubs in London teaching Aikido alone. Contemporary fashion photography in Britain has been strongly influenced by cult Japanese magazines. And consider also the impact of Buddhist philosophy, the everyday use of the concept of karma, the prevalence of Manga-influenced cartoons, and even the popularity of Muji 'no brand' stores.

East Asian culture is playing an increasingly important role in British society and as a result life in London is evolving. It's a more stimulating place for it.

SHOPPING

Oriental City
399 Edgware Road, NW9
0181 200 0009
One of the major Oriental shopping plazas in London with a food court, and stores selling Eastern crockery, clothing and publications. Also has a Japanese bookstore

Sogo (London Ltd)
228/229 Piccadilly, W1
0171 333 9000
Sogo has been a famous curiosity for Londoners since it opened in 1992. The large department store in Piccadilly catered mainly for Japanese tourists; supplying British goods in a Japanese-speaking environment. The economic downturn in the Far East has had a major impact and it has now been forced to close

Mitsukoshi
14 Regent Street, W1
0171 839 6714
Mitsukoshi has taken the place of Sogo – it too is a Japanese department store which stocks mainly European-style clothes in Japanese sizes – Burberry is a favourite – and accessories for Japanese tourists in London

Muji
187 Oxford Street, W1
0171 437 7503
Muji has tapped into the apparently insatiable desire of hip, 30-something, home-owning Londoners for Japanese-style, unbranded household goods and stationery. Every Saturday, the branches in central London are stuffed with shoppers seemingly unable to resist the translucent soap dishes and metallic notebooks

Ray Man Eastern Musical Instrument
29 Monmouth Street, WC2
0171 240 1776
An amazing variety of traditional musical instruments from China, Tibet, Malaysia and Thailand as well as from America and Africa

photographs: Julian Anderson

Guanghwa Company
7 Newport Place, WC2
0171 831 5888
From the street, Guanghwa appears to be a Chinese-language bookshop but the basement is a treat. Amongst the bric-a-brac, there are amazing Chinese artists' materials including rice paper, ink blocks, and bamboo and wolf hair brushes

OCS Books
2 Grosvenor Parade, Uxbridge Road,W5
0181 992 6335
Japanese-language books and some travel books in English

Japan Centre Book Shop
212 Piccadilly, W1
0171 439 8035
Publications on Japanese culture in English as well as Japanese language books

Charing Cross Library
4 Charing Cross Road, SW1
0171 641 4628
Because of its proximity to Chinatown, the Charing Cross Library has a substantial collection of Chinese-language books for loan

M Salon
29-30 Avery Row, W1
0171 499 0565
One of at least ten Japanese hairdressers in London. It offers head massages as well as sharp haircuts to Japanese and British clients

HEALTH

British Acupuncture Council
Park House, 206 Latimer Road, W10
0181 964 0222
Acupuncture has been central to traditional Chinese medicine for nearly 5000 years. It is claimed that inserting needles or applying heat or electrical stimulation to specific acupuncture points can unblock energy channels called meridians. Once the regular flow of energy is restored, the body can start to heal itself. Western

Muji, bringing Japanese style to London 30-somethings

explanations centre on the notion of stimulation of natural pain-relieving chemicals. The Council will supply a list of acupuncturists by area (as defined by postcode), or for £3.50 will send their complete register

The Centre for Traditional Chinese Medicine
78 Haverstock Hill, NW3
0171 284 2898
Practitioners of Chinese herbal medicine and shiatsu massage, with Tai Chi and Qi Gong meditation technique classes too

Yellow Dragon Centre
17-19 Lever Street, EC1
0171 251 8020
As well as teaching Daoism, Feng Shui, Meditation, Tantric Buddhism, Tai Chi, Qi Gung, and Kung Fu in classes and one-to-one, the Yellow Dragon centre also runs courses on 'Door Supervision' for bouncers (which covers restraining techniques and fire and safety regulations), and 'Soul Delivery' said to help those who died traumatically find favourable reincarnation. There is an open evening every Monday at 19:00 for those interested in what goes on

Register Of Chinese Herbal Medicine
PO Box 400, Wembley, Middlesex
07000 790332
The RCHM maintains a register of member practitioners – there are over 200 in London

Chinese Herbal Medicine Clinic
3 Station Parade, Burlington Lane, W4
0181 995 1355
Consultations on Chinese herbal medicine and acupuncture

Eastern Chinese Herbal Clinic
16 Fulham High Street, SW6
0171 731 7888
Consultations on Chinese herbal medicine

Chinese Medicine Centre
15 Little Newport Street, WC2
Crammed with banks of drawers and bottles of carefully-labelled Chinese medicinal herbs

PUBLICATIONS

Sing Tao (European edition)
Chinese language daily paper published in Britain
SiYu Life
Monthly Chinese-language lifestyle magazine published in the UK
Taipei – London newsletter
Newsletter for the Taiwanese community in London
UK Life
A paper for the Korean community
The Filipino
Bi-monthly magazine for the Filipino community in London
Eikoku News Digest, Journey, The Nichi-ei Times, UK Weekly, INFILE, London Zok Magazine
Publications which can be found in Japanese shops and restaurants

ORGANISATIONS

Daiwa Anglo-Japanese Foundation
13 Cornwall Terrace, NW1
0171 486 4348
Aims to enhance cultural understanding between Japan and the UK. It supports those wishing to establish links with Japan. Funds scholarships and grants for projects which will enhance British and Japanese citizens' mutual understanding

Singapore UK Association
Vice-President: Dr Tay
0171 377 7617

Korean, Mandarin and Japanese lettering are a common feature of London shopfronts

Holds social events, organises Singapore Golf Club and other celebrations for anyone with a connection to Singapore

The Japan Society
Suite 6/9, 6th Floor, Morley House, 314/322 Regent Street, W1
0171 636 3029
Organises cultural, social and educational events for members

The Japan Foundation
17 Old Park Lane, W1
0171 499 4726
The Foundation aims to promote culture and the Japanese language in the UK. It administers funding for films, books, TV documentaries and PhD research on Japan-related subjects. The affiliated London Language Centre at 27 Knightsbridge, SW1, is a key resource for people learning to teach Japanese in the UK. It also provides a forum for talks and discussions on Japanese culture by invited speakers

Great Britain China Centre
15 Belgrave Square, SW1
0171 235 6696
Holds Mandarin classes taken by those who have business with China, Cantonese-speaking Londoners who wish to learn Mandarin and people planning to spend some time in China. The Centre has a library and publishes *China Review* which includes a diary of Chinese arts-related events in the UK

SPORTS

World Tae Kwon Do
89 Sandringham Road, Worcester Park, Surrey
0181 395 7881
Originally a Korean martial art, Tae Kwon Do is now practised all over the world

Kyudo – Japanese Archery
Twyford Sports Centre, Twyford Crescent, W3
0181 993 9095
Historically, the bow has both a sacred and a functional significance in Japanese culture. The act of shooting a bow and arrow is seen to express beauty and truth. As the bow became obsolete as a weapon, the spiritual aspect of archery was developed in Kyudo as a discipline for peace and self-cultivation

Mumeishi Kendo Club
Cranford Community School, High Street, Cranford, Hounslow
0181 897 6609
Kendo evolved from the sword fighting techniques practised by the Samurai warriors. The sword is now substituted by a shinai – made up of four pieces of bamboo

Wu Shu Kwan
1 The Colonnades, Bishops Bridge Road, W2
0171 229 6354
A form of Chinese kick boxing, commonly known as Kung Fu

photographs: Julian Anderson

CO LTD
Con un colpo di reni al 90' se
Blair rilancia
la Repub
中國進入不穩定高峰
The Asahi
法施行から1年4カ月
LONDON'S
FREE-ADS
藝精品鐘
國際電話咭一律
NBA ACTION
CHICAGO BULLS
Sleeping with the enemy
THE X FILES MOVIE
EDDIE MURPHY
Rolatruc
SELF RAISING FLOUR

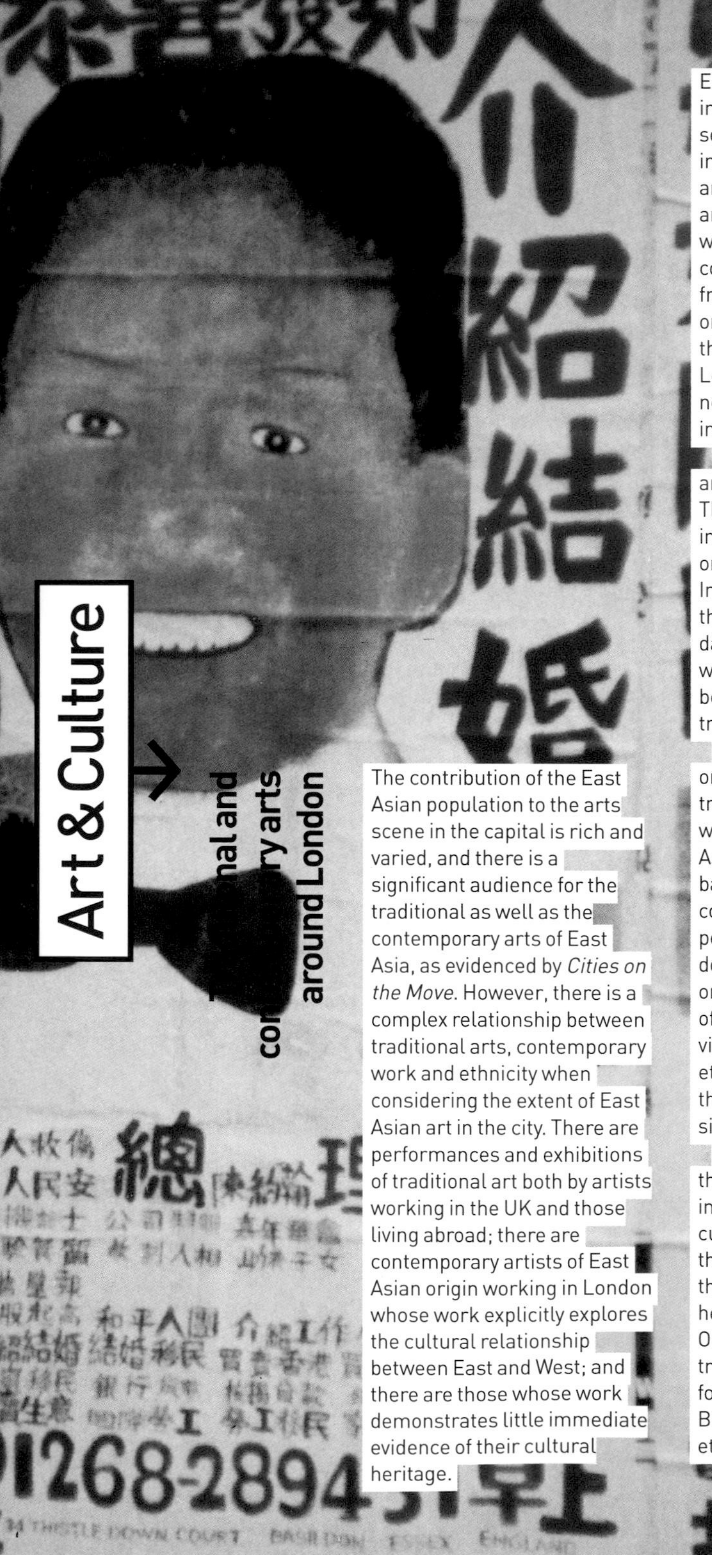

Art & Culture

…nal and co…ry arts around London

The contribution of the East Asian population to the arts scene in the capital is rich and varied, and there is a significant audience for the traditional as well as the contemporary arts of East Asia, as evidenced by *Cities on the Move*. However, there is a complex relationship between traditional arts, contemporary work and ethnicity when considering the extent of East Asian art in the city. There are performances and exhibitions of traditional art both by artists working in the UK and those living abroad; there are contemporary artists of East Asian origin working in London whose work explicitly explores the cultural relationship between East and West; and there are those whose work demonstrates little immediate evidence of their cultural heritage.

The traditional visual arts of East Asia are well represented in the permanent collections of some of the larger institutions in London, such as the V&A and the British Museum. There are also a number of galleries which specialize in work by contemporary artists from East Asia either resident or visiting, although much of the work of those living in London is shown in the many non-specialist galleries located in the city.

East Asian performing arts are equally well represented. The South Bank Centre, for instance, has its own Gamelan orchestra playing traditional Indonesian percussion, and there are several musical, dance and theatre groups which explore the fusion between Eastern and Western traditions.

But the real issue is that once we move away from the traditional arts, when does work by contemporary East Asian artists and performers based in London become contemporary British art or performance? At what point does categorization by ethnic origin become irrelevant and offensive? How does the artist view the significance of their ethnic origin in relation to their work? And what is its significance for us, the viewer?

The answer is, of course, that there is a dynamic interaction between the cultures of East and West in this city and this is reflected in the work of those who live here. Where there may be Oriental influence, we have tried to include it here. Decide for yourself whether it is British or not and whether its ethnic origin is significant.

photograph: Julian Anderson

East Asian performance in London is part of daily life. Bottom: Xi Ju Che Jian theatre company, part of LIFT (see p.88)

photograph: Anne Odling-Smee

Much of the work of contemporary East Asian artists and performers is not on permanent display and appears in mainstream venues some of which are listed here, along with a number of music, theatre and dance groups working in London, and some of the permanent collections kept in the capital.

MUSIC

The Thai Music Circle
c/o The Royal Thai Embassy
29 Queens Gate, SW7
0171 589 2944
Thai music is traditionally associated with the Thai Royal Court and musicians were attached to courts and aristocratic households. It can trace its roots back to the 14th century and, although it has been influenced by Chinese, Indian, Khmer, Burmese, Javanese and Malay musical traditions, it remains distinctly Thai. It utilizes an equiheptatonic musical scale which has no semitones. The Thai Music Circle aims to encourage appreciation of traditional Thai music amongst both the Thai community and Western audiences. It organises workshops and classes as well as pertomances

The UK Chinese Orchestra
0181 440 1664
e-mail: yc4@soas.ac.uk
The UK Chinese Orchestra is a group of six to ten professionial musicians from mainland China now living in the UK who perform traditional Chinese instrumental music. They also collaborate with musicians of other ethnic backgrounds to produce new work

Grand Union Music Theatre
380 Old Street, EC1
0171 729 8729
A group of musicians from around the world now living and working in the UK

Asian Music Circuit
Westpoint, Warple Way, W3
0181 742 9911
The Asian Music Circuit aims to bring some of the best musical groups from Asia to perform all over the UK, usually performing at the South Bank Centre when in London

Royal Festival Hall Gamelan Programme
0171 921 0848
The gamelan orchestra consists mainly of percussion instruments and often accompanies Indonesian shadow puppet shows which tell traditional stories originally from India. Each gamelan has its own tuning, preventing instruments from being interchanged from one gamelan to another

DANCE

Bima Dance Company
0171 383 3408
Contemporary Malaysian dance company which explores the fusion of Eastern and Western dance techniques

Barrio Fiesta
Lampton Park, Hounslow
Held on the second Sunday in July every year: entrance free
There are several Philippine fiestas over the summer, where there's dancing, food, handicrafts for sale. The Barrio Fiesta is the largest: normal attendance is over 20,000 people

THEATRE GROUPS

Yellow Earth Theatre
47 Croxley Road, W9
0181 968 4074
East Asian theatre group whose work explores the cultural duality of East and West

UK Chinese Acrobatic Company
27 Waltham Avenue, NW9
0181 204 3406
Chinese acrobatics date back to 475-221BC. The members of the UK Chinese Acrobatic Company were all professionally trained in China from as young as six years old. They perform lion dances, dragon dances, martial arts and hoop diving

ARTS ASSOCIATIONS

LIFT (London International Festival Of Theatre)
19-20 Great Sutton Street, EC1
0171 490 3964
Organises an international theatre festival held in venues around London every two years. 1999 is a LIFT year

Far Eastern Arts
6A Philip Lane, N15
0181 801 8628
Arranges performances of traditional and contemporary dance, music, singing and acrobatics from South East Asia, and exhibitions of the work of South East Asian artists

British Chinese Artists Association
0171 267 6133
Promotes work of British Chinese visual artists, performance artists and film makers. Call to receive a newsletter and updates on events around London

Asia House London
105 Piccadilly, W1
0171 499 1287
Asia House organises exhibitions and performances of traditional and contemporary work from the whole Asian region. A special programme for members includes lectures, gallery tours and visits

Institute of International Visual Arts (inIVA)
Kirkman House, 12/14 Whitfield Street, W1
0171 636 1930

A contemporary visual arts organisation with a special interest in new technologies, commissioning site-specific artworks and international collaborations. inIVA encourages new forms of collaboration with artists, curators and writers from culturally diverse backgrounds. Between May and September 1999, inIVA is organising a season of exhibitions and events entitled 'Post-Colonial Cities' which explores the dynamic of different urban experiences in the late 1990s

GALLERIES & MUSEUMS

Victoria & Albert Museum
Cromwell Road, SW7
0171 938 8500
The Indian and South East Asian Study Room at the V&A contains around 6,000 paintings. In addition, the gallery holds a number of collections of East Asian art, including the T.T. Tsui Gallery of Chinese Art, the Samsung Gallery of Korean Art and the Toshiba Gallery of Japanese Art, which is one of the largest permanent displays of Japanese art, design and craft outside Japan

British Museum
Bloomsbury, WC1
0171 636 1555
An extensive collection of Oriental antiquities including Chinese bronzes, jades, porcelain and paintings. The Joseph E. Hotung Gallery presents the history of China, South and South East Asia from prehistoric times through to the present with archeological material, objects of daily use, and religious sculptures. A new permanent Korean gallery opens in 2000 and will display examples of early Buddhist art from the 14th century

Wellcome Museum
The Science Museum, Exhibition Road, SW7
0171 938 8000
The Wellcome collection of the history of medicine can be found on the top floor of the Science Museum. Henry Wellcome was interested in the history of mankind and many of the items on display have only a tenuous connection with the history of medicine. Part of the collection is made up of Chinese and Japanese pieces from the 17th, 18th and 19th centuries including opium pipes, acupuncture needles and fascinating ivory diagnostic dolls – used by women to point out their symptoms so the doctor wouldn't have to touch them

Wallace Collection
Manchester Square, W1
0171 935 0687
The arms and armour collection contains some amazing examples of oriental weapons and suits of armour from the 18th and 19th centuries

Percival David Foundation of Chinese Art (SOAS)
53 Gordon Square, WC1
0171 387 3909
Collection of Chinese ceramics from the 10th to 18th centuries

Commonwealth Institute
Kensington High Street, W8
0171 603 4535
The Commonwealth Institute permanent collections have been gathered to reflect contemporary culture of the 54 commonwealth countries including textiles, ceramics, as well as art, games

photograph: Anne Odling-Smee

Opposite and right: LIFT performances from Japan and Bali (see p. 88)

and musical instruments. Currently closed for major redevelopment, the Institute reopens in 2002

Brunei Gallery
Thornhaugh Street, WC1
0171 323 6230
Specializes in South East Asian art

Chinese Contemporary Gallery
11 New Burlington Place, W1
0171 734 9808
This commercial gallery specializes in displaying work by contemporary artists from mainland China

The Horniman Museum
100 London Road, SE23
0181 699 1872
The often-overlooked Horniman Museum is undergoing some major changes. It has recently opened its new African Gallery and next year it opens a Collectors Gallery which will document the history of collecting. The original Horniman Asian collection will be displayed in the new gallery which includes a huge gilt Buddha from Japan

Daiwa Foundation Japan House
13/14 Cornwall Terrace, NW1
0171 486 4348
The regular in-house programme includes exhibitions of Japanese painting, pottery and sculpture. There are also concerts, performances, workshops and lectures. A library and information centre are open to the public from 09:30-16:30. Japan House is open daily from 09:00-17:00 and events are free. Regular meetings and events are also held here by the Japanese community organisations and societies

THEATRES & VENUES

SOAS
Thornhaugh Street, Russell Square, WC1
0171 637 2388
www.soas.ac.uk

BAC (Battersea Arts Centre)
176 Lavender Hill, SW11
0171 223 2223

Barbican Centre
Silk Street, EC2
0171 638 4141

Riverside Studio Theatre
Riverside Studios, Crisp Road, W6
0181 237 1000

Royal Festival Hall and Queen Elizabeth Hall
SBC, Belvedere Road, SE1
0171 960 4242

Sadlers Wells
Rosebery Avenue, EC1
0171 863 8000

Place Theatre
17 Dukes Road, WC1
0171 387 0031

CINEMA

Japanese Information And Cultural Centre (JICC)
Japanese Embassy, 101-104 Piccadilly, W1
0171 465 6500
Screens Japanese-made films

The Metro
Rupert Street
0171 734 1506
Frequently screens Hong Kong films

EXHIBITION EVENTS

In association with the staging of *Cities on the Move* in London, a series of talks, performances and events explore the Asian city as well as the relationship between East and West.

Reading Art

'This show is a stunning examination of the city as a living organism: the conurbations of the East as continually moving entities, subject to the influence of technology, machinery, traffic, consumerism and human wonder. In a great deal of traditional Far Eastern architecture structures were mobile: performance was against the sway of Buddhist philosophy. And so, in this exhibition, we see how traditional ways of thinking have tangled with the frenetic pulse of modern living. We see how cultural habits have been reshaped: in the noise of the city, the environment, the war of advertisements, the rise of tourism, and the daily attempts of people to inscribe themselves into the vast changeableness of Eastern urban space. "With cities", wrote Italo Calvino, "it is as with dreams: everything imaginable can be dreamed, but even the most unexpected dream is rebus that conceals a desire or, its reverse, a fear".'

Extract from *Cities on the Move*, an essay in celebration of the exhibition by writer-in-residence, Andrew O'Hagan. Complete essay available from Hayward Gallery Education.

Andrew O'Hagan

©Jeremy Young

Reading Art Talks – My kind of town

Saturday 26 June, 12 noon, 3pm, 5pm and 7.30pm
Voice Box, Royal Festival Hall
0171 921 0971

Readings, presentations and debates around the themes of cities and urban landscapes, curated by writer-in-residence Andrew O'Hagan. Speakers include Lawrence Chua, Anthony Cronin, Dave Haslam, Tom Leonard, Gordon Burn, Richard Sennett, Mary-Kay Wilmers and Deyan Sudjic.

Curators & Artists

Thursday 13 May, 7–9pm
Chelsfield Room, Royal Festival Hall

An evening presentation by Hou Hanru and Hans-Ulrich Obrist, curators of *Cities on the Move*, together with some of the exhibiting artists.
Tickets: £7.50, £5 members and concessions.*

Cities on the Move Conference

Friday 14 May, 10am–4.30pm
Chelsfield Room, Royal Festival Hall

Presentations and discussion sessions cover cultural politics, education, performance, film and architecture.
Organised in collaboration with Visiting Arts and Wimbledon School of Art.
Visiting Arts *Tickets*: £15, £12.50 members and concessions (includes entrance to the exhibition).*
*Special Joint Ticket covering both above events: £20, £15 members and concessions.

Cities on the Roof

Friday 14 May, doors 9.30pm
Queen Elizabeth Hall Roof

Late evening performance by Japanese turntable artist and musician, Otomo Yoshihide. This specially-created performance was commissioned as part of the music programme at the Royal Festival Hall.
Tickets: £10

Lantern by Lisa Cheung, leader of the City Lights project

Tuesday Gallery Talks

Tuesdays, 18 May–22 June, 6.30–7.30pm
Hayward Gallery

Speakers from a variety of specialisations give personal responses to the exhibition in a series of informal talks in the Gallery.
18 May Melanie Keen, project curator at inIVA
25 May Lewis Biggs, director of Tate Gallery Liverpool
1 June Ole Scheeren, exhibition co-architect, OMA
8 June Meg Rodger, art historian
15 June Fiona Bradley, exhibition organiser, Hayward Gallery
22 June Andrew O'Hagan, writer
Admission free with exhibition ticket for that day.

Gallery Guides

Wednesdays, 4–7.30pm
Sundays, 1–4pm
Hayward Gallery

British-based artists talk informally with visitors in the exhibition.

Hayward Forum

Dislocated Harmonies: Chinese Urban Life Today
Wednesday 2 June, 6.30–7.45pm
Hayward Gallery Pavilion

Chinese cities have long offered an aesthetic expression of social, ethical and philosophical visions. What is happening to the expressive order and the underlying reality of these cities today? If the density, variety, prosperity and dislocations of

Saburo Teshigawara in performance

Chinese urban life produce a new creative order, what will it symbolize?
Chair: Simon Glendinning (University of Reading)
Speakers: Nick Bunnin (Centre for Modern Chinese Studies, University of Oxford), Anthony Grayling (University of London)
Admission free with exhibition ticket for that day.

City Lights
Hayward Gallery Pavilion
Artist-in-residence, Lisa Cheung, leads the City Lights project, in which visitors to *Cities on the Move* are invited to make a lantern. Each lantern is displayed in the Gallery's Pavilion, extending into the Hayward sculpture court and lit up on the final day of the exhibition, Sunday 27 June at 9pm.
Lantern making: £1 materials charge in addition to exhibition ticket for that day.

Triad: Saburo Teshigawara in performance
Thursday 10 & Friday 11 June, 8.30pm
Hayward Gallery
A unique chance to see the work of leading Japanese dancer, choreographer, costume designer and sculptor, Saburo Teshigawara perform in the exhibition accompanied by the music of Merzbow.
Tickets: £10, £8.50 members and concessions

Video Wall
13 May–27 June, nightly 8pm–5am
Sainsbury's, Clapham High Road
A programme of video work by exhibiting artists, including Zhu Jia's film *Forever*, shot on a camera mounted on a tricycle wheel, is screened on a video wall at the Clapham branch of Sainsbury's.

Cities on the Move: the Billboard
Jubilee Gardens on the South Bank
13 May–27 June
Exhibiting Thai artists, Navin Rawanchaikul and Rirkrit Tiravanija have created a billboard painting for display within *Cities on the Move*. This painting incorporates images from Asia with those of the South Bank site and staff. This is the first stage in adapting the artists' original work – shown in previous galleries on the exhibition's tour – to reflect a sense of the local community and environment. The second stage will operate as a consultation process with artists, Lana Wong and Shona Illingworth, who will engage with a selection of representatives from businesses local to Jubilee Gardens, with the aim of encouraging them to share with us their views of this part of London. The resulting images and texts will be incorporated into a display of the new London poster.

salon3
Elephant and Castle Shopping Centre
Opens 14 May
A collaboration at salon3, a project space in a former television showroom in the Elephant and Castle Shopping Centre. Artists, architects, designers and film makers are invited to plug something into one of salon3's many electrical sockets, as a homage to the celebrated concept of the Plug-In City by architect Peter Cook of Archigram.
Selected by Rebecca Gordon Nesbitt, Hou Hanru, Maria Lind and Hans-Ulrich Obrist.

The infamous elephant at Elephant and Castle. salon3 is nearby

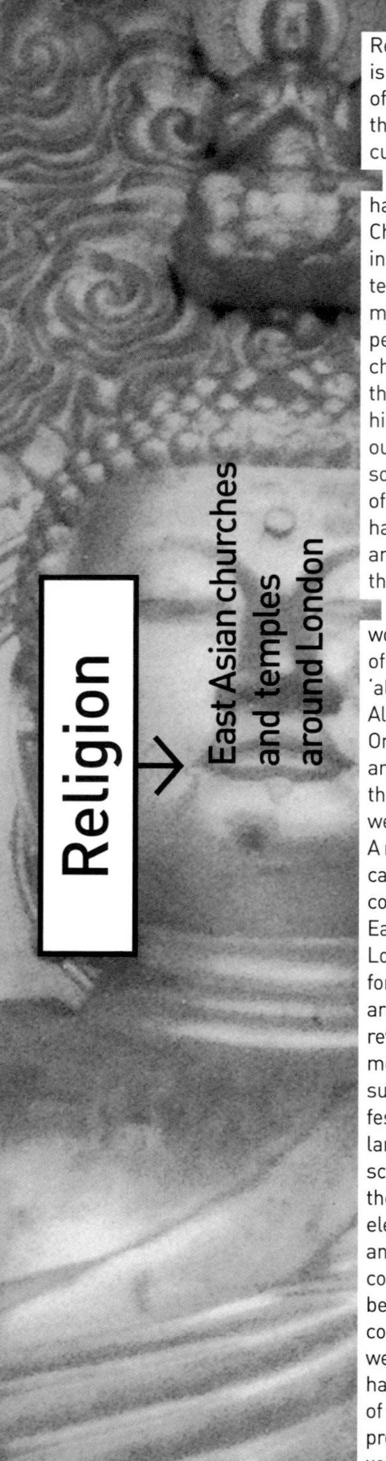

Religion

East Asian churches and temples around London

Religious belief, by definition, is one aspect of the presence of East Asians in London where there has been little cross-cultural fusion.

In a city whose landscape has for so long been defined by Christian churches, the introduction of Oriental temples and mosques has markedly changed our physical perception of the city. The church spire is juxtaposed with the minaret in many suburban high streets. For some, even in our secular, post-Christian society, the physical presence of East Asian religious centres has been the focus for tension, and has served to emphasize the cultural boundaries.

Non-Christian places of worship are concrete evidence of the permanent presence of 'alien' culture in London. Although the abundance of Oriental restaurants is arguably more highly visible, they derive their business from welcoming other cultures. A religious centre, in contrast, caters mainly for its congregation. Indeed, for some East Asian communities in London, temples and mosques form a cultural centre, a hub around which a community revolves. It provides a place to meet, to share ideas, to offer support. With social events, festivals, mother-tongue language classes, film screenings and exhibitions, they often act to preserve elements of the ethnic culture and provide a voice for the community. Whilst this is beneficial for minority communities in London, and welcomed by many others, it has also served to agitate some of the indigenous population providing a focus for xenophobic hostility.

However, just as it would be a massive over–simplification to suggest that the Anglican Church represents the beliefs of all Londoners, it would be equally naïve to suggest that the Oriental religions – Buddhism, Hinduism, Islam and others – represent the beliefs and practices of all East Asians in London. Western colonialisation in the 19th and 20th centuries and the dogged work of missionaries means that Christianity is also widely practised in East Asia and this is reflected in London. There are, for example, nearly as many Catholic Vietnamese as there are Buddhist Vietnamese; there's a Japanese Christian church in Acton; and the Catholic church in New Malden is a major community centre for Koreans living in the area.

It could be argued that the popularisation of Buddhist philosophy is evidence of cross-cultural exchange but its introduction to London was mainly by way of returning travellers rather than the presence of East Asians in the city.

London has been home to people of many different religious beliefs and has accommodated many architectural and cultural influences in its long history. With time, the temples and mosques will become assimilated into the cityscape and appear less alien. The city has a huge ability to embrace disparate cultures, claiming them for its own. The Oriental religions and the architecture of their places of worship have brought to London an enriching dimension.

The American Church
79A Tottenham Court Road, W1
0181 954 1890
Holds Chinese-language Christian services. Also offers interpreters or Japanese-speaking assistants for wedding blessings

Buddhapadia Temple
Thai Temple, 14 Calonne Road, SW19
0181 946 1357
Hidden deep in the leafy suburban streets of Wimbledon, the Thai temple acts as a focus for the local Thai community. It holds language classes and dancing lessons for children on Sundays as well as providing study in Buddhism. The Temple is open to the public at weekends from 13:00–18:00

Central Baptist Church
Aubyn Square, SW15
0181 876 4493
Holds Japanese-language services

Chinese Graves
East London Cemetery, Grange Road, E13
0171 476 5109
The first Chinese community in London was based in Limehouse. The pre-war Chinese community in the East End is commemorated by a stone cross erected in 1927 in the Western section of the cemetery

East London Mosque
84-92 Whitechapel Road, E1
0171 247 1357
With its three minarets, the East London Mosque which opened in 1985, is a strikingly beautiful sight amidst the scruffiness of the surrounding area

Japanese Buddhist (Souka-Gakkai) Temple
1, The Green, Richmond, Surrey
0181 948 0381

London Central Mosque and Islamic Cultural Centre
Regents Park, NW1
0171 724 3363

photographs: Julian Anderson

London Fo Kuang Shan (Temple) of Master Hsing Yon
84 Margaret Street, W1
0171 636 8394
Tucked away behind Oxford Street, the London Fo Guang Shan Buddhist Temple was established in 1992 by its parent monastery in Taiwan. The main shrine is on the first floor. There is also a meditation hall, a library which holds books, videos and audio tapes, a dining hall and a common room. Normal weekly services are held on Sunday mornings from 10:30

Lotus Temple, Buddhist-Korean Society
5 Waters Road, Kingston upon Thames, Surrey
0181 549 6092
The tiniest of Buddhist temples located in an ordinary suburban house in Kingston, distinguishable only by a small sign in the window

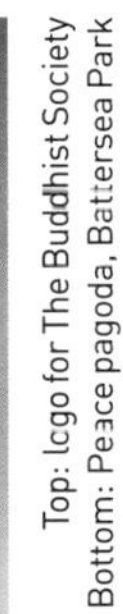

Top: logo for The Buddhist Society
Bottom: Peace pagoda, Battersea Park

The Korean Catholic Church
St Anne's Church, Kingston Vale, New Malden, SW15
0181 546 4013
With a congregation consisting of over 500 Koreans it is perhaps surprising that the church does not own a dedicated space. It operates by renting St Anne's Church for services at noon every Sunday. There is, however, a dedicated rectory and priest

Nichiren Buddhist Temple Of London
8 Irvine Court,
100 Whitfield Street, W1
0171 388 3693

Rhenish Church (UK)
1 Orange Street, W1
Chinese-language Christian services held in this little church behind the National Gallery

Shri Swaminar
Hindu Temple, Neasden
0181 965 2651
The Shri Swaminar is the first Hindu Temple to be built outside India in the traditional fashion in 800 years since those built in Angkor Wat, Cambodia. Set in the suburban landscape of Neasden, the Temple is a spectacular sight. It is open to people of all faiths every day from 09:00-18:00 for private worship. Although many Hindus from outside India have diffe rent names for the Hindu deities, the Shri Swaminar is the only Temple in London where all the main godheads have been consecrated. Communal prayers take place in the complex next door to the Temple

Shinto
Shinto is the indigenous religion of Japan and has the animistic beliefs of the ancient Japanese at its roots. It involves the private worship of the spirits. There is only one Shinto priest in the UK. He can be contacted through the Information and Culture Centre at the Japanese Embassy on 0171 465 6500

Top: Buddhist Temple, Wimbledon
Bottom: Lotus Temple, Kingston

WEBSITES

Chinatown Online
http://www.fresco-web.co.uk/chinatown
London's Chinatown website. Recipes, shops, horoscopes, explanations of Chinese traditions, and even a guide to find your local Chinese restaurant

Bangsawan – A Lost Art Form
sunflower.singnet.com.sg/hsh17/Sect2
Looks at the history of this Malaysian genre and how it has played an important role in the development of other South East Asian popular theatre styles

The Asian Art Shop
http://www.theasianartshop.com
The Asian Art Shop sells artifacts, food, and books from East Asia which can be bought on line. These include Thai Spirit Houses; the larger ones measure over 6ft by 2ft and cost US$2000

I Jing
www.facade.com/occult/iching
The I Jing is an ancient Chinese Daoist system which aims to give moral guidance on issues. It is usually performed by throwing three coins three times whilst focusing a question of importance. The pattern of heads and tales relates to pre-written points of guidance. This site does the casting of coins on line and then delivers the I Jing answer to your question

Japanese events in London
www.embjapan.org.uk
An up to date list of Japanese exhibitions, films, lectures and seminars all over London

Asian Music Circuit
www.amc.org.uk/asianmusic
Includes a national calendar of Asian-related musical events taking place in London and the UK

Eastern Arts Report Online
www.eapgroup.ndirect.co.uk
Lists exhibitions, reprints articles from the Eastern Arts Report, gives news and much more on Eastern arts in the UK

Institute of International Visual Arts
www.iniva.org
On-line commissioned work and exhibitions, talks, seminars from international artists in the UK

Artefact
www.artefact.co.uk
Details on 495 of Britain's art galleries and dealers exhibitions with lists of exhibition openings in London and the rest of the UK

Art & Arts
aix.webspace.co.kr/~arts
A multi-media database on contemporary Korean artists and their work

Asian Art
www.asianart.com
An on-line journal for the study and exhibition of Asian arts worldwide

Bali & Its Culture
www.indo.com/culture/culture.html
Comprehensive site on Balinese culture including food, religion, history, music, dance and arts

Cambodian Classic Dance
www.netaxs.com/~tskramer/dance.html
Khmer performing arts, especially courtly dance

Chinese Film
www.insidechina.com/china/culture
Part of an official Chinese government site which includes a look at contemporary Chinese film

Hmong Home Page
www.hmongnet.org
The history, language and culture of the Hmong people whose ancestral home is the upland regions straddling the borders of Vietnam, Laos, Thailand and Southern China

Gate Foundation International Art Agenda
www.base.nl/gate
International diary of activities and exhibitions relating to Asian art

Council of East Asian Libraries
darkwing.uoregon.edu/~felsing/jstuff/cinema.html
Links to Japanese performing arts and cinema websites

Japan Performing Arts Net (JPAN)
www.jpan.org
Covers background, history, and economics of the performing arts in Japan, including the relationship between contemporary and traditional dance

Joglosemar Online
www.joglosemar.co.id
Arts and culture of Central Java

Khmer Art treasures
sgwww.epfl.ch/BERGERl
Part of the Worldwide Arts Appreciation World Treasures site which contains photographs of Khmer art treasures

South East Asian Art & Culture
www.gunung.com.seasiaweb/index.html
A major resource for those interested in the arts and cultures of South East Asia including a rare look at Filipino art, architecture and performing arts

Taiwan culture
www.roc-taiwan.org/f_culture.html
An official Taiwanese website which includes some interesting details on traditional Taiwanese culture and festivals

Thai culture
www.mahidol.ac.th/Thailand
Exploration of Thai arts, religion, history, politics and classic dance

Daiwa Anglo-Japanese Foundation
www.daiwa-foundation.org.uk
A site dedicated to connections to Japan-related internet resources

Acupuncture
www.Acupuncture.com
Acupuncture and traditional Chinese medicinal techniques explained

BORN

Caudéron, France
Quanzhou, China
Shantou, China
Shanghai, China
Taipei, Taiwan
Jakarta, Indonesia
London, UK
Zhengzhou, China
Singapore
Strasbourg, France
Harvard, USA
Shizuoka, Japan
Basel, Switzerland
Hong Kong
Tokyo, Japan
Chiayi, Taiwan
Fujian, China
Oita City, Japan
Japan
Bangkok, Thailand
Japan
Taegu, Korea
Unchoen, Korea
Linz, Austria
Salzburg, Austria
Seoul, Korea
Rotterdam, The Netheralnds
Nagaya, Japan
Ayutthaya, Thailand
Yongwol, Korea
Guanghou, China
Jitra, Malaysia
Guangzhou, China
Vancouver, Canada
Kindberg, Austria
Genoa, Italy
Chang Mai, Thailand
Buenos Aires, Argentina
New York, USA
Kyoto, Japan
Florence, Italy
Ibaraki Prefecture, Japan
Pusan, Korea
Xian You, China
China
Baguio City, Philippines
Stuttgart, Germany
Braunschweig, Germany
Bandung, Indonesia
Singapore
Indonesia
Shiga, Japan
Galle, Sri Lanka
Liantang Village, China
Japan and Scotland
Hubei, China
Sichuan Province, China
Penang, Malaysia
Wuhan, China
Kobe City, Japan
Penang, Malaysia
Beijing, China
Hangzhou, China
Yiangjiang/Guangzhou, China

Arahmaiani
Paul ANDREU
Nobuyoshi ARAKI
Shigeru BAN
Duangrit BUNNAG
CAI Guo-Qiang
Yung Ho CHANG
CHEN Shaoxiong
CHEN Zhen
CHI Ti-Nan
Heri DONO
EDGE
FOREIGN OFFICE
Anne FRÉMY
GENG Jianyi
Simryn GILL
Dominique GONZALEZ-FOERSTER
HANAYO
HARVARD-PROJECT
Itsuko HASEGAWA
David D'HEILLY
Kayoko OTA
HERZOG & DE MEURON
Oscar HO
Richard HO
Tao HO
Takashi HOMMA
HUANG Chin-ho
HUANG Yong Ping
Arata ISOZAKI
Toyo ITO
Lucas JODOGNE
Sumet JUMSAI
Chitti KASEMKITVATANA
KAY Ngee Tan
KHOO Eric
Kiyonori KIKUTAKE
Jimai KIM
Soo-Ja KIM
KIM Yun-Tae
Takeshi KITANO
Karl Heinz KLOPF
Aglaia KONRAD
KOO Jeong-A
Rem KOOLHAAS
Kisho KUROKAWA
Susasi KUSOLWONG
LEE Bul
LIANG Juhui
LIEW Kung Yu
William LIM
LIN Yilin
Armin LINKE
LIU Thai Ker
Ken LUM
Greg LYNN
Fumihiko MAKI
Fiona MEADOWS
Frederic NANTOIS
Sohn-Joo MINN
Ryuji MIYAMOTO
Rudi MOLACEK
Mariko MORI
Takashi MURAKAMI
Matthew NGUI
Tsuyoshi OZAWA
Ellen PAU
Renzo PIANO
Eko PRAWOTO
Cedric PRICE
Navin RAWANCHAIKUL
Rirkrit TIRAVANIJA
Jesse REISER
Nanako UMEMOTO
Richard ROGERS
Kazuyo SEIJIMA
SEUNG H-SANG
SHEN Yuan
SHI Yong
Judy Freya SIBAYAN
Matt GATTON
Marintan SIRAIT
Andar MANIK
Yutaka SONE
Margherita SPILUTTINI
Manit SRIWANICHPOOM
SUPERFLEX
Aaron TAN
Fiona TAN
Takahiro TANAKA
TAY Kheng Soon
Chandraguptha THENUWARA
TSANG Tsou-choi
USHIDA FINDLAY
WANGDu
WANG Jian Wei
WANG Jia Qiang
Jun-Jieh WANG
WONG Hoy Cheong
WONG Kar-Wai
WONG & OUYANG
XU Tan
Riken YAMAMOTO
Miwa YANAGI
Ken YEANG
YIN Xiuzhen
YUAN Shun
ZHAN Wang
ZHANG Peili
ZHENG Guogu
ZHOU Tiehai
ZHU Jia

LIVE

Port Dickson, Malaysia
Shanghai, China
Taipei, Taiwan
Yogyakarta, Indonesia
Paris, France
Hangzhou, China
Harvard, USA
Tokyo, Japan
Basel, Switzerland
Hong Kong
Taichung, Taiwan
Bangkok, Thailand
Seoul, Korea
Brussels, Belgium
Everywhere
Rotterdam, The Netherlands
Guangzhou, China
Kuala Lumpur, Malaysia
Milan, Italy
Vancouver, Canada
Los Angeles, USA
New York, USA
Perth, Australia
Sydney, Australia
Genoa, Italy
London, UK
Fukuoka, Japan
Manila, Philippines
Bandung, Indonesia
Vienna, Austria
Copenhagen, Denmark
Amsterdam, The Netherlands
Singapore
Sri Lanka
Zuhai, China
Berlin, Germany
Beijing, China
Hangzhou, China
Yangjiang, China